Editorial Project Manager
Lorin E. Klistoff, M.A.

Managing Editor
Karen J. Goldfluss, M.S. Ed.

Illustrator
Mark Mason

Cover Artist
Brenda DiAntonis

Art Production Manager
Kevin Barnes

Art Coordinator
Renée Christine Yates

Imaging
James Edward Grace

Publisher

Mary D. Smith, M.S. Ed.

Authors

Mary Tucker and Kim Rankin

Teacher Created Resources, Inc.
6421 Industry Way
Westminster, CA 92683
www.teachercreated.com
ISBN-13: 978-1-4206-7059-2

© *2007 Teacher Created Resources, Inc.*
Made in U.S.A.

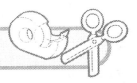

Table of Contents

Introduction

Many of children's favorite Bible stories which they love hearing again and again are found in the New Testament. How can we make these stories fresh so they will hold children's attention when they have heard them so often? In this book, each story is presented in a creative way, using methods that will capture and hold children's attention. Methods include the following: interviews, pantomimes, action rhymes, walk-abouts, skits, telling the story with simple props or objects, drawing sketches on the board, and much more. Even familiar stories, such as Jesus' birth, will come alive for children when you use these methods.

This book is also filled with fun crafts, one to accompany each story. Children will enjoy making the crafts, and the results will be something they will be proud to take home to share with their families. The crafts are designed to use easily obtainable items such as the following: construction paper, colored markers, glue, craft sticks, felt, paper or plastic plates, foil, paper bags, glitter, yarn, etc. Clear, step-by-step directions are provided for each craft, as well as any reproducible patterns you will need.

Most of the Bible stories are old favorites, but a few are less familiar ones your children should get to know. Accompanying each story are discussion questions to help the teacher show children how to apply the truths of the story to their lives. Also included is a correlated memory verse to help with the personal life application. (*Note:* This book uses the *New International Version* of the Bible.) The stories are presented in a way that will help children understand them and see God at work in the lives of people. The storytelling methods often call for student participation, since children learn best when they are involved.

Each Bible story and craft can stand on its own and may be taught consecutively or selected at random. As children learn these wonderful stories of Jesus and His followers and create the crafts which reinforce the stories, may they realize that God loves being closely involved in people's lives, helping, teaching, and enabling them to do His will.

 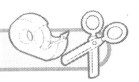

A Visit from an Angel

Bible Story: Matthew 1:18-24

As you tell the story of Joseph's dream, pantomime the action and have students do the same.

In the town of Nazareth lived a man named Joseph, a carpenter. Joseph was engaged to be married to a young woman named Mary from the same town. But there was a problem—Joseph had found out that Mary was pregnant! "Oh no," thought Joseph, "how terrible!" *(Put hand over mouth and look shocked.)* He knew he was not the father of her baby, so he decided not to marry her after all. This decision made Joseph very sad because he loved Mary. *(Look sad.)* Mary had told Joseph that her pregnancy was through the Holy Spirit. An angel had appeared to her and told her who was going to give birth to the Son of God! Who would ever believe such a crazy story? Joseph didn't. *(Shake head "no.")*

Then one night Joseph had a strange experience. As he was sleeping, he had a dream. *(Rest head in hands as if sleeping.)* In his dream an angel of the Lord spoke to Joseph. "Joseph, son of David," the angel said to him, "don't be afraid to make Mary your wife. The baby growing inside her really is the Son of God. *(Put your hand on your stomach, then point to heaven.)* When the baby is born, you are to give Him the name Jesus because He will save people from their sins." The name Jesus actually meant "the Lord saves."

Suddenly, Joseph woke up. *(Sit up straight and stretch and yawn.)* He must have sat on his bed wondering if he was asleep or awake. *(Slowly shake your head in confusion.)* Had he only dreamed that an angel had spoken to him or did it really happen? Joseph realized that an angel really had spoken to him. Now, he knew that Mary had told him the truth about her baby. *(Shake your head "yes.")*

Joseph got out of bed and went to see Mary. *(Stand up and walk in place.)* He apologized to Mary for not believing her. He asked her to marry him, and she said "yes." *(Shake your head "yes.")* Joseph did not waste any time. He and Mary became husband and wife, and she went to live with him at his house.

Joseph did not care what the other people in Nazareth thought. He and Mary knew the truth. God had specially chosen them to be the earthly parents of His Son! They had been reading the Scripture and looking forward to the day when God would send His Son, the Messiah, to the earth. *(Hold hands out like an open book.)* They were happy to be a part of God's plan.

Joseph was glad to have Mary as his wife. He knew God would bless their marriage. He would do exactly what God told him and raise Jesus as his own son. *(Raise hands and face to heaven.)*

A Visit from an Angel

Discussion

- Why do you think God spoke to Joseph through an angel in his dream?
- How did Joseph show that he believed that God could do the impossible?
- To whom else did the angel speak? *(Mary)*
- Why was it important for Joseph to know the right name to give God's Son?
- God proved He could do the impossible when He had His Son be born on the earth. Read the verse below. What are some other ways God has shown that nothing is impossible for Him?

Memory Verse

"For nothing is impossible with God." (Luke 1:37)

Craft Materials

- patterns on pages 6 and 7
- white cardstock
- crayons, markers, or colored pencils
- glue sticks
- scissors

Craft Directions

1. Copy the patterns on cardstock.
2. Color and cut out the pictures.
3. Fold in the sides of the card where indicated. This will hide the verse.
4. Glue the angel to the left side of the folded flap of the card as shown.
5. Open the card to memorize the verse.

Finished Product

Angel Pattern

"For nothing is impossible with God." Luke 1:37

Jesus Is Born

Bible Story: Luke 2:1-20

Divide students into two groups—shepherds and angels—to read this poem. You can read the part of the narrator or choose a good reader to do it.

Narrator:	Caesar Augustus decided to take a census of everyone.
	Each one had to go to his home town and sign up.
	Joseph and Mary left their home and traveled to Bethlehem.
	When they got there, the inn was full, but God had a place for them.
	They went to a stable and Mary gave birth to God's Son right there in the hay.
	Who would have guessed that the Lord of all would be born in such a way!
Shepherds:	We were out in the fields guarding our sheep on that quiet night
	When suddenly up in the sky we saw an angel—oh, what a sight!
One Angel:	Don't be afraid. I have good news. God's Son has been born for you.
	In Bethlehem, in a manger He sleeps. Go, and see that it's true.
Angels:	Glory to God in the highest heaven and on the earth below!
	Peace to men everywhere on Earth on whom God's love is shown.
Shepherds:	The angels suddenly disappeared, and we left our sheep and ran
	To Bethlehem to find God's Son who had come to Earth for man.
	We found Him in a manger bed sleeping peacefully.
	Then we hurried off to tell everyone what we had heard and seen.
Narrator:	Everyone was amazed to hear the shepherds' exciting story
	As they thanked their holy God above and gave Him praise and glory.
All:	Many years have passed since then, but we all know it's true—
	That God's Son, Jesus, came to Earth to die for me and you.

Jesus Is Born

Discussion

- What is a census? *(When a country counts all its people and gathers information about them.)*
- How did God show He was watching over Mary and Joseph?
- Why did the angel say he had good news for the shepherds?
- Why do you think God chose to send His Son to the earth as a baby instead of a grown man?
- Read the memory verse below. Who is "the Word" in this Bible verse? *(Jesus)* God is a spirit, but Jesus came to the earth and was born with flesh like any other person. What does it mean when it says He "made his dwelling among us"?

Memory Verse

"The Word became flesh and made his dwelling among us." (John 1:14a)

Jesus Is Born

Craft Materials

- patterns on pages 10 and 11
- white cardstock
- crayons, markers, or colored pencils
- glue
- scissors
- wood craft sticks *(optional)*
- yarn *(optional)*

Craft Directions

1. Copy the patterns on cardstock.

2. Color and cut out the patterns.

3. Glue the manger legs to the manger. For a unique craft, glue wooden craft sticks to the back of the manger. (If you use large wooden sticks, they will need to be cut in half, or you can purchase the 2 1/2" size.)

4. Cut small pieces of yarn for the hay, and glue them on the manger.

5. Glue baby Jesus to the manger as shown.

Finished Product

Baby Pattern

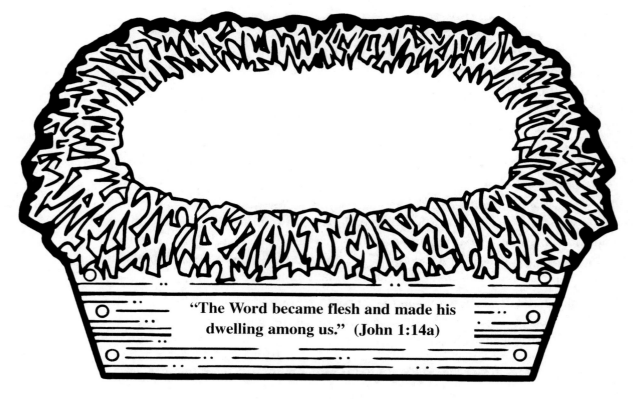

"The Word became flesh and made his dwelling among us." (John 1:14a)

Manger Pattern

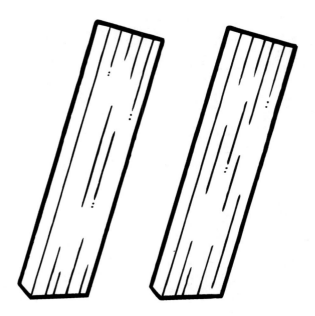

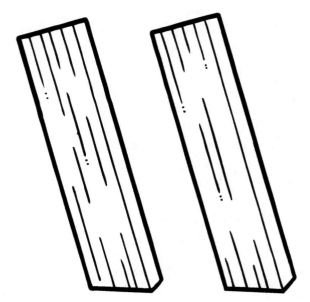

Manger Legs

Wise Men Worship Jesus

Bible Story: Matthew 2:1-15

Since this story is familiar to most children, let them help you tell it by answering the questions you ask.

When Jesus was born, whom did the angels tell first? *(shepherds)* The shepherds eagerly ran to the stable to see Baby Jesus, then they went out and told everyone they met that they had seen God's Son. When we see pictures of Jesus' birth or we look at nativity scenes at Christmas, we usually see three wise men and camels mixed in with the shepherds worshiping Baby Jesus. But the truth is that the wise men did not arrive to see Jesus until he was about two years old. By that time, Mary and Joseph had found a house to live in, so they did not have to be in the stable with the animals anymore. Here is why it took the wise men so long to get to Bethlehem.

How did the wise men know that Jesus had been born? *(They saw a special star in the east.)* Somehow the wise men were able to see God's message of Jesus' birth in that star. Apparently though, the star did not appear to them until Jesus was born. They set out for the land of Israel where they knew from their studies that the Messiah would be born. We do not know exactly what country the wise men were from, but it was far away. They had a long trip to make to find Jesus.

When they got to Jerusalem, the wise men stopped at the king's palace to look for the king. Where else would a new king be born? The wise men asked King Herod where they could find the King of the Jews, another name for Jesus. The king was upset to hear that there was a new king somewhere in his kingdom. He did not want any competition. He called the Jewish chief priests and teachers of the Law to find an answer for the wise men. They found it in the book of Micah the prophet. What town did Micah say would be Jesus' birthplace? *(Bethlehem)*

When the wise men left to go to Bethlehem, only a few miles away, King Herod invited them to stop by again on their way home. He said he wanted to know more about the new king so he could worship him, too. Actually, Herod wanted to find out where Jesus was so he could kill him!

Did the wise men find Jesus? *(yes)* What did they do when they found Him? *(They bowed down and worshiped Him, then gave Him gifts.)* What did they give Him? (Gold—which only rich people had; incense—a sweet smelling perfume sometimes used in medicines and also burnt in the temple to make a pleasant smell; and myrrh—the sweet smelling, gummy substance from a plant, often used to prepare a dead body for burial) These seem like strange gifts to give a two-year-old boy, don't they? Some people who have studied the Bible think that Joseph may have sold the gifts to get money to take Mary and Jesus to Egypt when they had to leave Bethlehem.

(Continued on the next page.)

Wise Men Worship Jesus

Bible Story: Matthew 2:1-15 (cont.)

We do not know for sure how many wise men came to see Jesus. We always show three of them because the Bible lists three gifts that they gave. But, there may have been more.

Before the wise men left, God warned them in a dream not to stop to see Herod on their way home, so they went back a different way. Then an angel of the Lord spoke to Joseph in a dream. He warned Joseph that King Herod was going to kill Jesus if he could find Him. The angel told Joseph to take his family to the land of Egypt and to stay there until he told him it was safe to go home. So, in the dark of night, Joseph led Mary and Jesus out of Bethlehem and headed for Egypt.

God was carefully watching over His Son on the earth and protecting Him.

Discussion

- Why do you think the wise men were so interested in finding Jesus?
- What do you think they said to Mary and Joseph and Jesus when they found them in Bethlehem?
- How did God take care of Jesus?
- The wise men were so happy to find Jesus—they knelt down and worshiped Him as soon as they saw Him. Read the memory verse below. This verse tells us to bow down to worship Him. What are some other ways we can worship the Lord?

Memory Verse

"Come, let us bow down in worship, let us kneel before the Lord our Maker." (Psalm 95:6)

Craft Materials

- patterns on pages 14 and 15
- white cardstock
- crayons, markers, or colored pencils
- glue sticks
- scissors

Craft Directions

1. Copy the patterns on cardstock.
2. Color and cut out the patterns.
3. Fold the card on the line to hide the verse.
4. Glue the wise men to the front of the flap.
5. Then glue the star to the top right side of the card as shown.

Finished Product

Star Pattern

Wise Men Pattern

"Come, let us bow down in worship, let us kneel before the Lord our Maker." (Psalm 95:6)

Fold line.

Jesus at the Temple

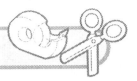

Bible Story: Luke 2:41-52

Choose students to act out this Bible story skit. You will need the following characters: 12-year-old Jesus, Mary, Joseph, two religious teachers, and four or five fellow travelers. You can read the part of the narrator.

Narrator:	Once a year Mary and Joseph traveled from Nazareth to Jerusalem to celebrate the Feast of the Passover, a Jewish holiday. When Jesus was 12 years old, they took Him with them. They traveled with a group of other people for safety. *(Joseph, Mary, Jesus, and the fellow travelers walk slowly around the room together.)*
Narrator:	Finally, they got to Jerusalem for the celebration. *(Joseph, Mary, Jesus, and the fellow travelers walk around excitedly as if gazing at all of the interesting sights, then bow on their knees and worship.)*
Narrator:	After the celebration was over, they started back home. *(Joseph, Mary, and the fellow travelers walk slowly back the way they came, not noticing when Jesus sits down with the two teachers.)* The travelers were a whole day away from Jerusalem when Mary and Joseph realized they had not seen Jesus. They looked everywhere for him, asking the other travelers about Him. *(Joseph and Mary frantically question the other travelers and look around.)* Nobody knew where Jesus was. Mary and Joseph headed back to Jerusalem, horrified that they had left their son behind in the big city all by himself.

Mary/Joseph: *(Mary and Joseph hurry back along the path and look for Jesus.)* Have you seen our son? Where can He be? Let's go look at the temple; maybe He's there. *(They hurry to the temple and find Jesus. He doesn't notice them until they speak to Him. Then He stands up.)* There He is! Oh, thank God! Jesus!

Mary: Son, why have you treated us like this? Your father and I have been searching for You everywhere!

Jesus: *(confused)* Why were you looking for Me? Didn't you know I would be here in My Father's house?

(Continued on the next page.)

Jesus at the Temple

Bible Story: Luke 2:41-52 (cont.)

Teachers:	We are amazed at this boy's understanding of God's Word
Joseph:	Thank you for the time you have spent with Him. Come, Jesus. It is time to go home now. *(Joseph, Mary, and Jesus leave and slowly walk toward home.)*
Narrator:	The little family went home to Nazareth. Jesus had not meant to cause trouble for His parents. He had no idea they would not know where to find Him. He obeyed them in every way, but there were some things about Him that His earthly parents never understood. As Jesus grew up, He not only grew physically and mentally; He also grew wise and people approved of Him. He never misbehaved nor did wrong things. He never mistreated people. He did what was right. And God, His true Father, was pleased with Him.

Discussion

- Why do you think Jesus loved being at the temple talking to the religious teachers?
- Should Mary and Joseph have been angry with Jesus? Why or why not?
- Why do you think Jesus' parents didn't understand some things about Him?
- How was Jesus different from other boys?
- Read the verse below. Jesus grew up the same way you're growing up. He grew physically, which means He gained weight and grew taller and became a strong man. He grew in wisdom, which means He not only gained knowledge, but He also learned how to make right choices and how to treat other people the way God wanted. He grew in favor with God and men, which means God and other people approved of the way He behaved. How are you growing in these four ways?

Memory Verse

"Jesus grew in wisdom and stature, and in favor with God and men." (Luke 2:52)

Jesus at the Temple

Craft Materials

- patterns on pages 18 and 19
- white cardstock
- crayons, markers, or colored pencils
- glue sticks
- tape
- scissors

Craft Directions

1. Copy the patterns on cardstock.

2. Color and cut out the patterns.

3. Use tape to hinge the left hand side of the door. This will allow the door to open freely to reveal the verse inside.

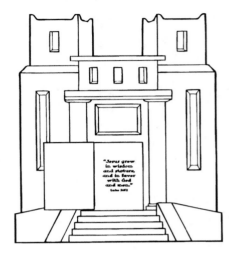

Finished Product

Door Pattern

Jesus grew
in wisdom
and stature,
and in favor
with God
and men.

(Luke 2:52)

John the Baptist

Bible Story: Matthew 3

As you tell this Bible story, draw simple pictures on the board and have students copy them on paper to illustrate the main points

Before Jesus became well known, another man had everyone's attention. His name was John; we call him John the Baptist. *(Draw a stick figure man.)* There were no church denominations back then, so we do not call him by that name because he went to a Baptist church. We call him that because he baptized so many people. A better name for him would be John the Baptizer.

John was Jesus' cousin, and God sent him to prepare the way for His Son. John was an unusual man with a strong message that he was not afraid to tell anyone who came near. He spent his time in the wilderness, in the desert of Judea. He wore rough camel hair clothing. *(Draw a hairy robe on the stick figure.)* He did not care about having nice, comfortable clothes to wear. He did not care about having fancy meals to eat either. He ate mostly locusts and wild honey. *(Draw locusts flying around John.)* Locusts were insects like big grasshoppers, often eaten by poor people. John found the wild honey in hollow trees. *(Draw a hollow tree.)*

Crowds of people came from nearby villages and cities to see John because they were curious about him. *(Draw a crowd of stick figure people.)* Was he a wild man? When they heard him preach, they realized he was not a wild man, but a prophet of God. His message was, "Repent of your sins now, for the Messiah, God's Son, is coming soon."

Many people listened to him and did what he said. When they confessed their sins and believed, John baptized them in the Jordan River. *(Draw wavy lines for water.)* Some people thought maybe John was the Messiah, but he assured them he was not. He told them that the one who was coming was so much better than him, he was not fit to even fasten His sandals!

Sometimes John's truthfulness made people uncomfortable or angry. When Jewish religious leaders came to hear him preach, he called them poisonous snakes and warned them that they needed to repent of their sins like everyone else. You can imagine how unpopular this made him with the religious leaders!

One day as John was preaching, Jesus came to be baptized by him. *(Draw another stick figure.)* "Oh no," said John, "I can't baptize you. I need for You to baptize me!" John knew that Jesus had never sinned, so He did not need to repent and be baptized. But Jesus insisted, and John agreed to do what He asked.

(Continued on the next page.)

John the Baptist

Bible Story: Matthew 3 (cont.)

They walked into the river, and John baptized the Son of God like he had baptized many other people before Him. *(Draw the two stick figures in the river.)* But this time, something very special happened! When the baptism was over, heaven opened and John saw a dove flying down. *(Draw a bird flying toward the Jesus stick figure.)* It was the Holy Spirit in the form of a dove. The dove perched on Jesus and a voice from heaven said, "This is my Son whom I love. I am well pleased with Him." God had given His approval of Jesus, His Son.

Jesus was not baptized because He needed to be. He was baptized to begin His public ministry. And even though He had never sinned, Jesus wanted to set an example for people to be baptized.

Discussion

- Why do you think the Jewish religious leaders came to hear John preach?
- Why didn't John baptize the Jewish religious leaders?
- What did John mean when he told people they needed to "repent" of their sins?
- Read the memory verse below. Why do you think John called Jesus the Lamb of God? *(Explain to students that priests often offered lambs for burnt sacrifices for people's sins. Jesus came to be like those lambs, to give His life to pay for people's sins.)*

Memory Verse

"The next day John saw Jesus coming toward him and said, 'Look, the Lamb of God, who takes away the sin of the world!'" (John 1:29)

Craft Materials

- crayons, markers, or colored pencils
- patterns on pages 22 and 23
- white cardstock
- glue sticks
- scissors

Craft Directions

1. Copy the patterns on cardstock.
2. Color and cut out the patterns.
3. Glue John the Baptist and the verse in place as shown.
4. Glue the dove to a craft stick.
5. Cut a slit near Jesus' head (see line on pattern).
6. Insert the dove and move it back and forth.

Finished Product

John the Baptist

"The next day John saw Jesus coming toward him and said, 'Look, the Lamb of God, who takes away the sin of the world!'" John 1:29

Verse Pattern

Dove Pattern

John the Baptist Pattern

Glue the verse here.

Jesus Chooses Disciples

Bible Story: Matthew 4:18-22; 9:9-13; 10:1-4

Present the Bible story as an interview. Choose students to read the parts of Peter and Andrew, James and John, and Matthew. Let the rest of the group be the other disciples. You can be the interviewer. Use a toy microphone or make one by wrapping foil around a stick.

Interviewer:	Our special guests today are Jesus' disciples, His special students. The first disciples He chose were Peter and Andrew. How did you two meet Jesus, Andrew?
Andrew:	Peter and I were net fishing when Jesus came walking along the shore. I recognized Him right away. I had met Him before and told Peter about Him.
Peter:	He called out to us to follow Him. He said he would make us fishers of men.
Interviewer:	What did you do?
Peter:	We stopped fishing and went with Jesus. We walked with Him down the beach to where James and John were.
Interviewer:	Tell us what happened when you met Jesus, John.
John:	James and I were in our boat with our dad fixing our fishing nets, getting ready to go fishing when Jesus spoke to us.
James:	He told us to follow Him, and we did. We left our father in the boat and became Jesus' disciples.
Interviewer:	Matthew, where were you when you met Jesus?
Matthew:	I was at my tax booth; I was a tax collector. Jesus walked up to me and said, "Follow me."
Interviewer:	Did you know who He was?

(Continued on the next page.)

Jesus Chooses Disciples

Bible Story: Matthew 4:18-22; 9:9-13; 10:1-4 (cont.)

Matthew: Yes, I had heard about the amazing miracles Jesus had performed and the stories He told. I was thrilled to be asked to join Him in His work.

Interviewer: Jesus chose 12 men to follow Him and help Him while they learned what He wanted to teach them about serving God. Besides Peter, Andrew, James, John, and Matthew, He chose Philip, Bartholomew, Thomas, James son of Alphaeus, Thaddaeus, Simon the Zealot, and Judas. *(facing the rest of the group)* Did you learn a lot in the three years you followed Jesus?

Disciples: *(Individuals give various enthusiastic answers.)* Oh yes. It was amazing! Definitely!

Interviewer: Jesus' disciples traveled with Him from town to town, watching Him heal people who were blind and lame and sick with disease. He even gave life back to people who were dead! The disciples often did not understand the things He told them, and their faith wavered back and forth. But they learned from Jesus how to love God and people and how to serve God by serving people.

Discussion

- Why do you think Jesus chose fishermen to be His helpers instead of well-educated teachers or lawyers or religious leaders?
- Did all of Jesus' disciples learn what Jesus wanted to teach them? *(No, Judas never understood what Jesus was teaching them and he ended up betraying Him.)*
- The disciples were able to walk with Jesus and watch Him work and hear Him teach. Since Jesus is no longer living on the earth as He was then, how can we learn from Him?
- Read the memory verse below. What did Jesus mean when He said He would make His followers "fishers of men"? Are those who follow Him today "fishers of men"?

Memory Verse

"'Come, follow me,' Jesus said, 'and I will make you fishers of men.'" (Matthew 4:19)

Craft Materials

- patterns on pages 26 and 27
- white cardstock
- crayons, markers, or colored pencils
- glue sticks
- tape
- scissors
- sand

Finished Product

Craft Directions

1. Copy the patterns on cardstock.
2. Color and cut out the patterns.
3. Tape the boat at the top only, over the verse.
4. Apply glue to the beach area and sprinkle sand all over the beach.
5. Lift up the boat to read the Bible verse.

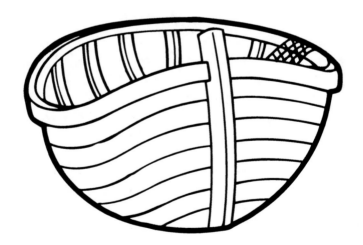

Boat Pattern

A Centurion's Faith

Bible Story: Matthew 8:5-13

Copy the figures of Jesus and the centurion on page 29 on cardstock for students to color and cut out. Provide craft sticks they can glue on the back of the figures for handles. As you tell the Bible story, let them act it out with the figures.

One day, a centurion came to see Jesus to ask for help. A centurion was an officer in charge of 100 soldiers in the Roman army. "Lord," he said, "I have a servant at home who is paralyzed. He is suffering terribly."

Jesus said to him, "I'll go and heal him." He saw that the centurion was a man of compassion who cared more for his servant than most people would have.

"No, no!" exclaimed the centurion. "I do not deserve for You to come to my house." The centurion was a Gentile and probably knew that Jewish law said that Jews were never supposed to set foot in a Gentile's home. The Jewish religious leaders would not even walk on the same side of the street as a Gentile! But Jesus never followed foolish rules like that. It was not one of God's rules, so He ignored it. He did not care if the man was a Jew or a Gentile; He just wanted to help him.

"If You just say the word," the centurion said to Jesus, "I know my servant will be healed. You are so powerful, You do not have to be there in the house to heal Him."

Jesus was amazed that a Roman soldier believed in Him that much. "I haven't found anyone in Israel who has as much faith as this centurion has," Jesus said. Then he told the man to go and what he had asked for would be done. The centurion's servant was healed at that very hour.

Discussion

- Why do you think the centurion came to ask Jesus to help his servant?
- How did Jesus show that He cared for the centurion and his servant?
- Read the memory verse below. What do you think this Bible verse means? Did the centurion live by faith or by sight?

Memory Verse

". . . if you have faith as small as a mustard seed, you can say to this mountain, 'Move from here to there' and it will move. Nothing will be impossible for you." (Matthew 17:20b)

Centurion Pattern

Jesus Pattern

Craft Materials

- patterns on pages 30 and 31
- white cardstock
- crayons, markers, or colored pencils
- glue sticks
- tape
- scissors
- hole punch
- yarn
- small zipped bag or cellophane
- mustard seeds (or other small garden seeds)

Finished Product

Craft Directions

1. Copy the patterns on cardstock.
2. Color and cut out the patterns.
3. Glue the verse on the empty bookmark
4. Place seeds in a zipped bag or in a pocket made from cellophane, taping the ends closed.
5. Tape the bag between the two bookmarks.
6. Glue the bookmarks together, back to back.
7. Use a hole punch to make a hole in the top of the bookmark and insert yarn for a tassel.

Variation: Do not cut out holes in the bookmark, just glue seeds around the edge.

> "... if you have
> faith as small as
> a mustard seed,
> you can say to this
> mountain, 'Move
> from here to there'
> and it will move.
> Nothing will be
> impossible for
> you."
> (Matthew 17:20b)

Verse Pattern

Bookmark Patterns

Cut out.

FAITH

Cut out.

Glue verse here.

Bible Story: John 5:1-15

Present this Bible story as a news report with interviews of those involved. Choose a good reader to be the reporter. You will also need the following characters: news anchor, blind person, two Jews, and a disabled man.

News Anchor: This is a special report on an exciting event that took place today in the city of Jerusalem. Let's go to our reporter who is at the Pool of Bethesda to find out what happened.

Reporter: I am here at the Pool of Bethesda near the Sheep Gate. All around me are disabled people hoping to be cured. They come here every day—the blind, the lame, the paralyzed—to get into the water which is said to provide healing when it is stirring. Most of them never experience healing, but today one man did. However, his healing did not come from the pool! The man had been an invalid for 38 years, but not anymore! Today he is walking around, healthy and strong. Surprising? It certainly is. Even if a man who can't walk is healed, legs that haven't been used for 38 years would be too weak to stand on. But not for this man. That is because the disabled man was healed by Jesus, the miracle worker! Let's talk to this sightless person who was here when the healing took place.

Blind Person: That's right; I was over there. Of course, I couldn't see what happened since I'm blind, but I could hear everything.

Reporter: What happened?

Blind Person: Jesus came up to my friend and talked to him. He found out how long he had been unable to walk. Then Jesus said to him, "Do you want to get well?" I thought to myself, "That's a silly question. Who wouldn't want to get well?"

Reporter: What did the disabled man say?

Blind Person: He explained that he did not have anyone to help him get in the pool when the water was stirring. Other people always got ahead of him. Then Jesus told him to get up, pick up the mat he was lying on, and walk!

Reporter: And was your friend able to walk?

Blind Person: Yes! I wish I could have seen him when he took those first steps. But I could hear him walking around. It was amazing!

Reporter: Here come a couple of men who spoke to the man after his healing. Excuse me, do you have time to speak to our TV audience?

Two Jews: Certainly, certainly.

Reporter: You saw the man healed here today?

(Continued on the next page.)

Bible Story: John 5:1-15 (cont.)

Jew One: Well, no, we did not actually see him healed. We saw him a few minutes later, carrying his sleeping mat.

Reporter: What did you say to him?

Jew Two: We reminded him that it was the Sabbath and he should not be carrying his mat!

Jew One: That is against Jewish law, you know.

Jew Two: He wasn't even sorry that he was breaking the law! He just told us that a man had told him to pick up his mat and walk, and that's what he had done.

Jew One: We asked him who told him that, but he did not know the man's name. We found out later that it was Jesus!

Reporter: Well, the important thing is that the man was healed. Right?

Two Jews: *(angrily)* The important thing is that he broke the law!

Reporter: Yes, well, thank you for taking time to talk to us. Look, there is the man who was healed! Excuse me! Sir? Are you the disabled man?

Disabled Man: *(smiling)* Not anymore!

Reporter: We heard that you had been healed. Your legs seems to work very well for someone who did not use them for 38 years. How do you feel?

Disabled Man: I feel great! I just met Jesus, the one who healed me, at the temple. He changed my life! *(runs off)*

Reporter: Well, I guess he is too excited to talk anymore. That's the news from the Pool of Bethesda here in Jerusalem.

News Anchor: What a wonderful story! And that wraps up our report. Good night!

Discussion

- Why do you think Jesus asked the disabled man if he wanted to be healed?
- When Jesus saw the man later, he told him to stop sinning or something worse might happen to him. What do you think Jesus meant?
- Read the verse below. How did the Lord show His compassion on the disabled man at the pool? How has the Lord shown compassion on you?

Memory Verse

"The Lord is gracious and righteous; our God is full of compassion." (Psalm 116:5)

Healing by a Pool

Craft Materials

- patterns on pages 34 and 35
- colored construction paper
- hole punch
- tape
- scissors
- yarn

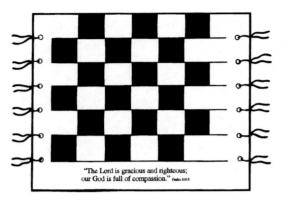

Finished Product

Craft Directions

1. Copy the patterns on colored construction paper.

2. Cut out the patterns.

3. Cut the dashed lines on the mat (card).

4. Weave the strips of paper in and out of the the slits. Tape the top and bottom of each one as you go.

5. Use a hole punch to punch holes where indicated on the mat. Insert strips of yarn for a tassel.

Paper Strip Patterns

Weaving Mat Pattern

O - O

O - O

O - O

O - O

O - O

O - O

**"The Lord is gracious and righteous;
our God is full of compassion."** Psalm 116:5

Jesus Feeds 5,000

Bible Story: John 6:1-15

Sing the Bible story song together to the tune of "When Johnny Comes Marching Home Again."

Great crowds of people followed Jesus everywhere
To watch Him heal the sick and show His loving care.
Upon a mountainside one day, the people would not go away,
So He fed 5,000 with some fish and bread.

A little boy gave Jesus what he'd brought for lunch,
Not nearly food enough to feed that hungry bunch.
But Jesus had them all sit down for a picnic on the ground.
And He fed 5,000 with some fish and bread.

Jesus prayed, then passed the bread and fish to all.
He multiplied the food from that one lunch, so small.
Everybody ate until everybody had his fill,
When He fed 5,000 with some fish and bread.

"Gather up what's left," He said when they were done.
They got twelve baskets more than what they had begun.
The people who'd seen everything wanted to make Him their king,
When He fed 5,000 with some fish and bread.

Jesus Feeds 5,000

Discussion

- Why do you think the people wouldn't go home when it was mealtime?
- Why do you think Jesus prayed before passing out the bread and fish to the people?
- Why did the people want to make Jesus their king?
- Read the memory verse below. Which of your needs is Jesus unable to meet? How has He met your family's needs? Give specific examples.

Memory Verse

"And my God will meet all your needs according to his glorious riches in Christ Jesus."
(Philippians 4:19)

Craft Materials

- patterns on pages 38 through 41
- white cardstock
- crayons, markers, or colored pencils
- glue sticks
- tape
- scissors

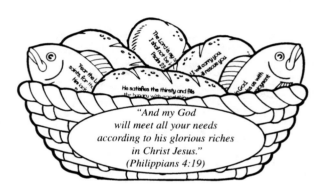

Finished Product

Craft Directions

1. Copy the patterns on cardstock.

2. Color and cut out the patterns.

3. Fold the basket in half and tape the sides to form a pocket.

4. Glue the Bible verse on the front as shown.

5. Fold the fish and loaves of bread in half and tape the tops. Make sure you can read the verses on the outside of each pattern.

6. Use the fish and loaves to memorize the verses.

7. Place the fish and loaves in the basket to keep them for later use.

 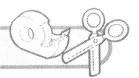

Jesus Feeds 5,000

Fish Patterns

"Fear the Lord, you his
saints, for those who
fear him lack nothing."
Psalm 34:9

Hope in God, who richly
provides us with everything
for our enjoyment.
1 Timothy 6:17b

Jesus Feeds 5,000

Basket Pattern

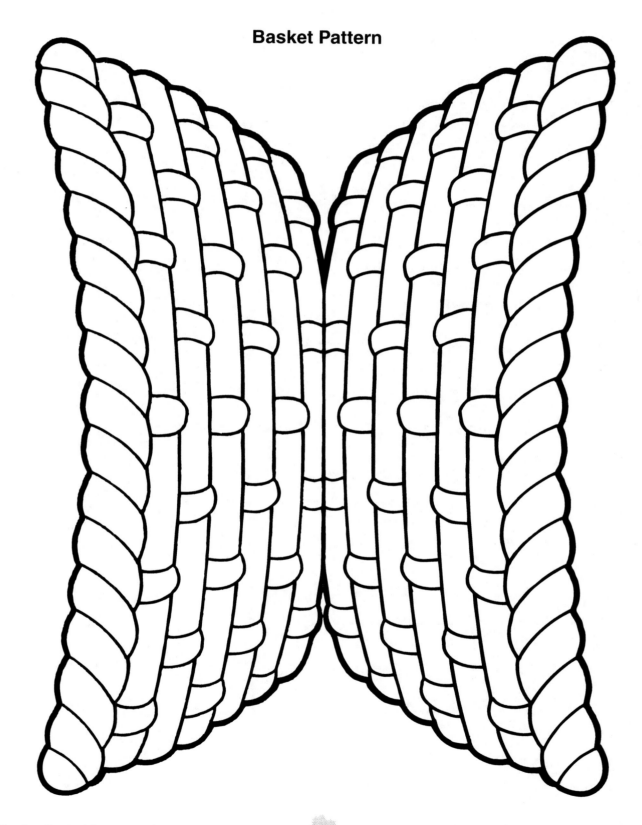

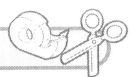

Jesus Feeds 5,000

Bread Patterns

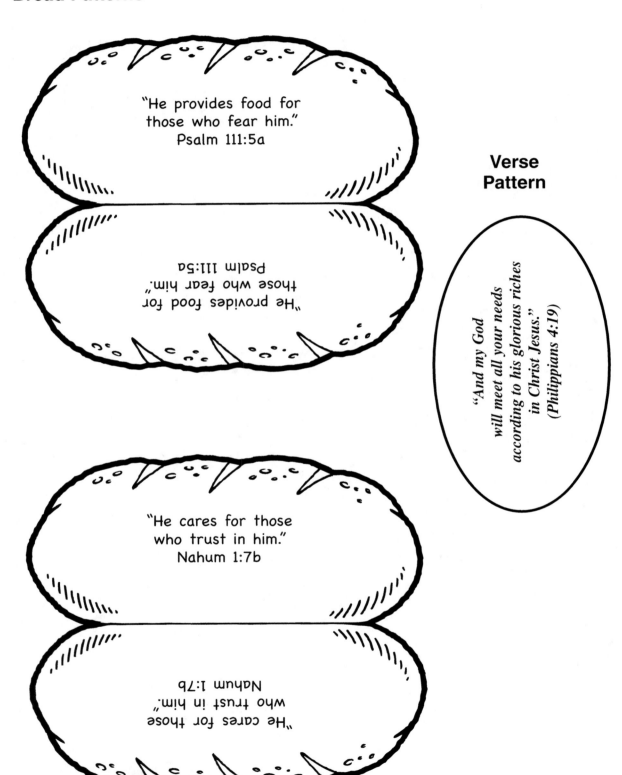

"He provides food for
those who fear him."
Psalm 111:5a

"He provides food for
those who fear him."
Psalm 111:5a

"He cares for those
who trust in him."
Nahum 1:7b

"He cares for those
who trust in him."
Nahum 1:7b

**Verse
Pattern**

"And my God
will meet all your needs
according to his glorious riches
in Christ Jesus."
(Philippians 4:19)

Bread Patterns

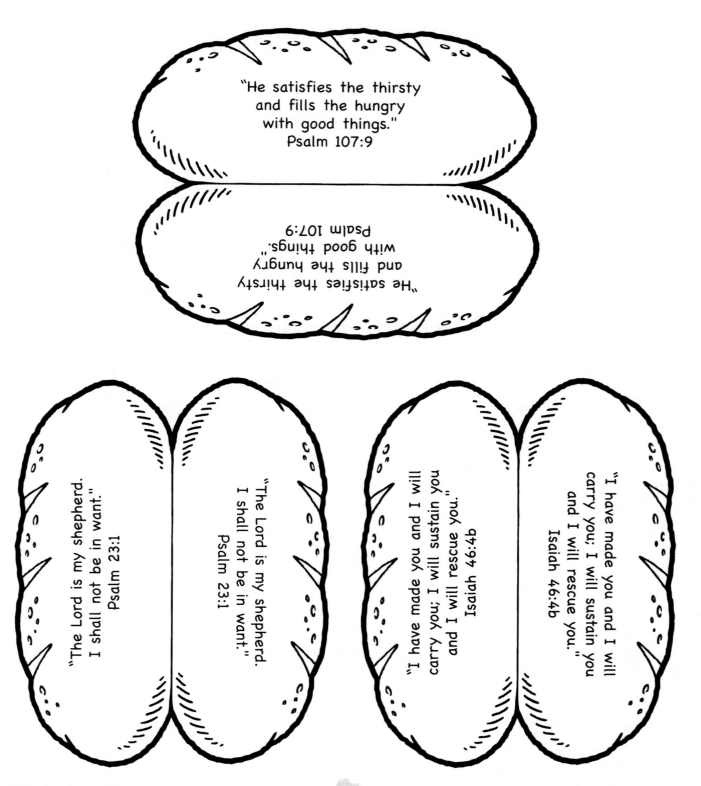

"He satisfies the thirsty
and fills the hungry
with good things."
Psalm 107:9

"He satisfies the thirsty
and fills the hungry
with good things."
Psalm 107:9

"The Lord is my shepherd.
I shall not be in want."
Psalm 23:1

"The Lord is my shepherd.
I shall not be in want."
Psalm 23:1

"I have made you and I will
carry you; I will sustain you
and I will rescue you."
Isaiah 46:4b

"I have made you and I will
carry you; I will sustain you
and I will rescue you."
Isaiah 46:4b

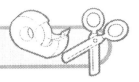

The Sower and His Seed

Bible Story: Matthew 13:1-9, 18-23

As you tell the Bible story, use the actions as noted and have your students copy you.

Often Jesus told stories, called parables, to help people understand important lessons. One day He was on the lakeshore talking to a crowd of people. More people came and soon there were so many, Jesus could not be seen and heard by all of them. He got into a boat and went out into the water a little way so they could all hear what He had to say. He told them this story.

A farmer went out to scatter seed in a field. *(Throw arm out as if you are sowing seeds.)* Some of the seeds fell along a path where the dirt was packed down, so the seeds just stayed on top. Birds came and quickly ate them. *(Pretend to be a bird pecking at seeds in your hand.)* Some of the seeds fell into dirt that had more rocks in it than soil. Because the dirt was so shallow, later on, when the seeds began to grow they did not have good roots. When the sun came out it scorched the weak plants and they withered and died. *(Shiver and move your body toward the ground as if withering or drying up.)* Some of the seeds landed among thorny weeds. There just wasn't enough room for them to grow because the thorns crowded them out. *(Hold your arms tight against your sides and look around as if at a crowded area.)*

However, some of the seeds landed on good soil. It was not packed down; it was crumbly and rich. It was not full of rocks or weeds, but there was plenty of room for the seeds to sprout and the plants to grow big and strong. *(Squat down, then slowly raise your joined hands above your head and stand up like a plant growing tall.)* The farmer had an excellent crop from those seeds.

Later, Jesus' disciples asked Him about the parable. They did not understand what Jesus was trying to teach in the story of the farmer and his seed. Jesus explained that the seed represents God's Word. *(Hold your hands out like an open Bible.)* The farmer's field represents the world. *(Make a big circle with your arms.)* The seed that fell along the path represents someone who hears or reads God's Word, but does not understand it because the devil is at work in his life. *(Hold out your hands and shrug your shoulders.)* The seed that landed in rocky soil represents someone who hears or reads God's Word and seems to be interested, but his interest does not last. His mind is filled with too many other things to give much thought to God. *(Point to your brain.)* He never lets the Word touch his heart. *(Put your hand over your heart.)*

(Continued on the next page.)

The Sower and His Seed

Bible Story: Matthew 13:1-9, 18-23 (cont.)

The seed that landed among thorny weeds represents someone who hears or read God's Word but lets other people or things keep him away from it. There just isn't room in his life for God. *(Hold out both hands in a stop gesture.)*

The seed that fell on the good soil represents someone who hears or reads God's Word and understands it, letting it touch both his mind and heart. *(Point to your brain, then your heart.)* He believes what it says and obeys it because he loves God. *(Point to heaven.)*

Jesus knew, when He came to the earth, that only a few people would believe in Him and accept Him. He realized that most people did not want to bother with reading God's Word or obeying it. He knew the devil would make many people think God's Word was not important and they could not understand it. Jesus wanted them to trust Him instead of going their own way, to understand that God loved them and wanted to change their lives.

Discussion

- God wants everyone to read His Word and believe it. What are some things that keep people from doing this?
- Why do you think people have a hard time trusting God when they don't understand something?
- Read the memory verse below. What do you do when you read something you don't understand in the Bible? What should you do?

Memory Verse

"Trust in the Lord with all your heart and lean not on your own understanding." (Proverbs 3:5)

Craft Materials

- patterns on pages 44 and 45
- cardstock
- crayons, markers, or colored pencils
- glue and/or glue sticks
- scissors
- variety of dried seeds and/or beans
- small paper plate *(optional)*
- glitter *(optional)*
- hole punch
- yarn

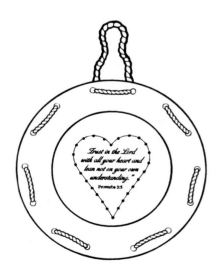

Finished Product

Craft Directions

1. Copy the patterns on cardstock paper.
2. Color and cut out the patterns.
3. Glue them in place on the circle or use a paper plate.
4. Use glue to attach larger seeds around the heart. Spread a thin layer of glue on the outer part of the heart and sprinkle on seeds.
5. Punch holes in the outer circle.
6. Weave yarn through the holes for a hanger.

Heart Pattern

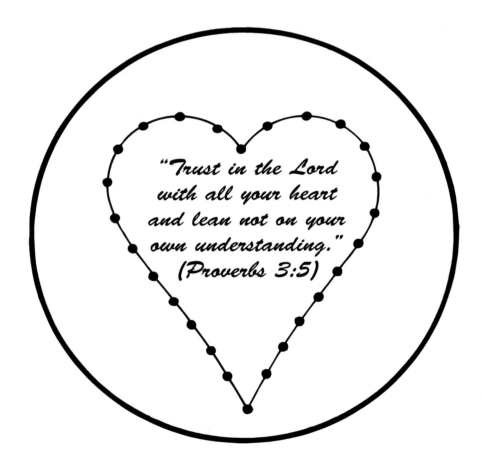

"Trust in the Lord with all your heart and lean not on your own understanding." (Proverbs 3:5)

The Sower and His Seed

Circle Pattern

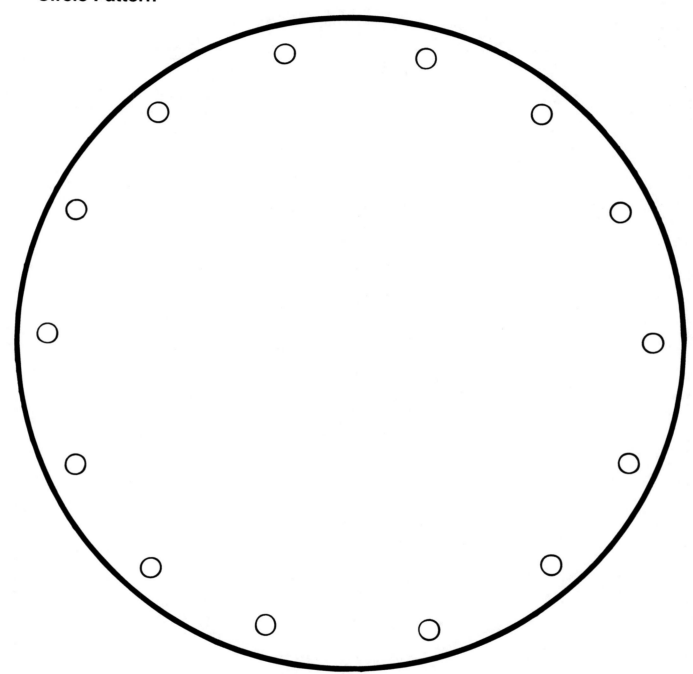

You can use this pattern instead of the paper plate.

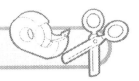
Bible Story: Luke 7:11-17

Read the Bible story rhyme and do the actions. Encourage your students to do the actions with you.

Jesus went to a town called Nain and what did He meet?

(Walk in place, then shade your eyes with your hand and look around.)

A man's funeral procession going down the city street.

(Shake your head sadly and point to something nearby.)

The people walked slowly by as they carried the man to his tomb.

(Walk slowly with lowered head and hands up as if carrying the casket.)

His mother cried for her son was dead, and her heart was filled with gloom.

(Pretend to cry.)

She was a widow and her son had been her only family alive.

(Put your face in your hands and shake your head sadly.)

What would she do now that he was dead? How would she survive?

(Hold your hands and face toward heaven as if asking for help.)

As the widow's sad friends carried her dead son slowly by,

(Walk slowly with lowered head and hands up as if carrying the casket.)

Jesus' heart went out to the mom and He said to her, "Don't cry."

(Hold out your arms as if comforting someone.)

(Continued on the next page.)

A Widow's Son

Bible Story: Luke 7:11-17 (cont.)

He knew that He could help her as no one else could do.

(Gesture to everyone with your arm as you shake your head "no.")

He walked up and touched the coffin and said, "I say to you,

(Walk in place, then reach out your hand as if touching something.)

Get up!" And all the people gasped as the dead man took a breath!

(Gasp in surprise and put your hand over your mouth.)

He sat right up and began to talk, full of life, not death.

(Stand up straighter and move your mouth as if talking.)

The widow was thrilled when Jesus gave her back her only son.

(Laugh and do a happy dance.)

The people praised the Lord and spread the news to everyone.

(Hold your hands up and praise the Lord.)

Discussion

- The woman in this story loved her son, so of course she was sad when he died, but why else was she so sad about his death? *(In Bible times women rarely held jobs, so they depended on their husbands or families to provide for them. With her son dead, the widow had no one to take care of her.)*

- How did the people in the funeral procession, and probably people standing along the road, respond when Jesus brought the dead man back to life?

- How has Jesus "carried" or "rescued" you and your family?

Memory Verse

"I have made you and I will carry you; I will sustain you and I will rescue you." (Isaiah 46:4b)

A Widow's Son

Craft Materials

- patterns on pages 48 through 50
- white paper
- crayons, markers, or colored pencils
- glue sticks
- scissors

Craft Directions

1. Copy the patterns on pages 48–50.

2. Color and cut out the patterns.

3. Glue the patterns on pages 49 and 50 back to back. Page 49 should be the inside of card and page 50 should be the outside of card.

4. Fold on the dashed lines. These are the flaps of the card. The sad woman and coffin should be on the outside, and the happy woman and Jesus with the boy should be on the inside.

5. Open the card to reveal Jesus and the boy.

6. Glue the verse in place.

**Finished Product
(outside of card)**

Verse Pattern

"I have made you and I will carry you; I will sustain you and I will rescue you."

Isaiah 46:4b

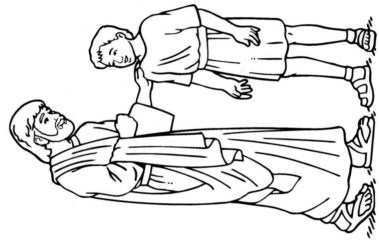

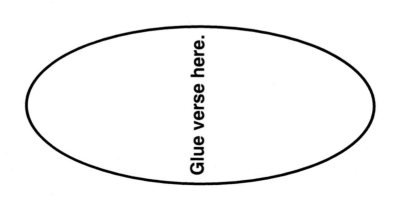

Glue verse here.

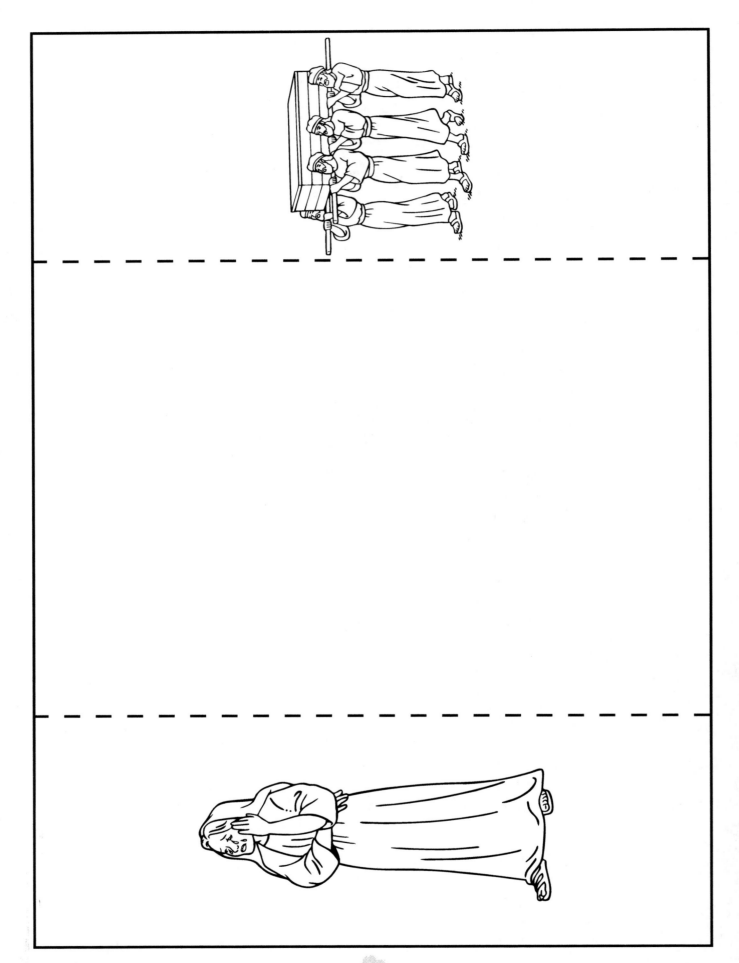

Jesus Calms the Storm

Bible Story: Luke 8:22-25

Before you tell the Bible story, place a rug on the floor for students to sit on and pretend they are in a boat, or arrange their chairs in a boat shape. Choose one student to act the part of Jesus. Begin the story with students standing up, not yet in the boat.

One day Jesus said to His disciples, "Let's go over to the other side of the lake." *(Have the student playing Jesus face the others and point far off.)* They all got into a boat and set off across the water. *(Seat students on the rug or in the chairs. "Jesus" should curl up in a corner of the boat and pretend to sleep.)* Jesus was so tired, he fell asleep.

Suddenly, the waves on the lake began to get bigger and the wind began to blow hard. The waves began tossing the boat around like a cork! *(Have students rock back and forth as if in a rocking boat and pretend to hold on to one another or the sides of the boat.)* Storms often hit the lake without warning, and some of the disciples were fishermen who had been through storms before. But this storm was so violent, it scared even the experienced fishermen! Back and forth, up and down over the choppy water they went. *(Students continue to rock back and forth.)* As the waves hit the sides of the boat, water splashed over the disciples and lay in pools in the bottom of the boat. They tried dumping the water out, but it did not do much good. They were afraid the boat was going to go down. *(Have students pretend to be splashed by waves, then dump water out of the boat.)* If the boat sank, they would not have a chance. They were too far from shore to swim, and who could swim in such a storm?

(Continued on the next page.)

Jesus Calms the Storm

Bible Story: Luke 8:22-25 (cont.)

Throughout the storm, while the disciples were fighting against the wind and waves, Jesus was calmly sleeping. Didn't He know what was happening? Why wasn't He doing something to help? The disciples woke Him up and said, "Master, we're going to drown!" *("Jesus" stands up and stretches, then calmly holds out his arms over the lake.)* Jesus got up and spoke to the wind and the waves. "Quiet! Be still!" He said. *(Mark 4:39)* Suddenly, the wind and waves quieted and the storm was over. The boat floated calmly on the lake as if there had never been a storm! *(Students stop rocking the boat and look around them, surprised.)*

"Where is your faith?" Jesus asked His disciples. *("Jesus" faces the others as if asking them a question.)* Didn't they know they were safe when they were with Him?

The disciples could not believe what had just happened. "Who is this?" they asked. *(Students look at Jesus and point at Him in amazement.)* "He commands even the winds and the water, and they obey Him." They had seen Jesus perform miracles to heal people, but this was the first time they had seen that He even had power over nature. Who else could speak to wind and water and make them do what he said?

Discussion

- Why do you think Jesus did not wake up when the storm hit?
- Why did the wind and waves obey Jesus?
- Why were the disciples fearful when they saw what Jesus did?
- Read the memory verse below. Throughout the Bible, stories are told of the miracles God performed, sometimes through people such as Moses and Elijah, sometimes on His own, and sometimes through Jesus. What is your favorite miracle in the Bible? Why? Does God still perform miracles today?

Memory Verse

"You are the God who performs miracles; you display your power among the peoples." (Psalm 77:14)

Jesus Calms the Storm

Craft Materials

- patterns on pages 53 through 56
- white paper
- crayons, markers, or colored pencils
- glue sticks
- tape
- scissors

Finished Product

Craft Directions

1. Copy the patterns on pages 53–56.

2. Color and cut out the patterns.

3. Cut along the top of the water line that is above the dashed line.

4. Glue the patterns on pages 54 and 55 back to back. Page 54 should be the outside of the card and page 55 should be the inside of the card.

5. Fold the card in half. (The water should form peaks on the top of the card when folded as shown at the top right side of this page. When the card is opened, the verse should be at the top and Jesus with calm waters should be at the bottom.)

6. Tape the right side of the boat pattern to the front of the card on the right bottom side. This is a flap. When opened, it should reveal the words, "Trust in the Lord."

7. Glue the verse to the inside of the card where indicated.

Verse Pattern

"You are the God who
performs miracles;
you display your power
among the peoples."

Psalm 77:14

TRUST
in the Lord!

54

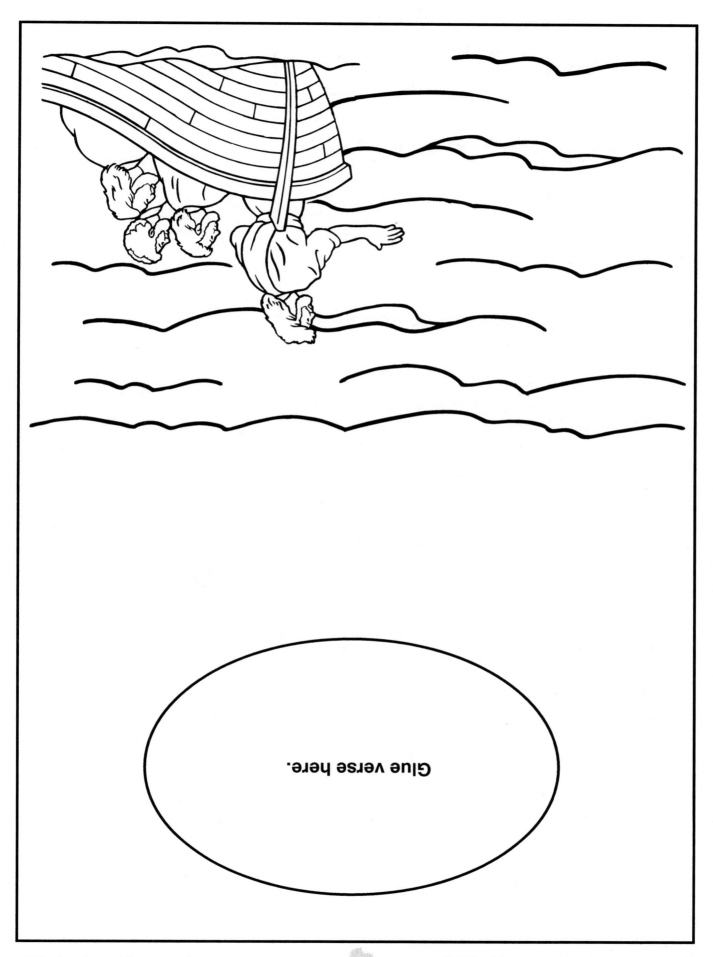

Glue verse here.

Boat Pattern

Jesus Walks on Water

Bible Story: John 6:16-21

Copy the Bible story poem for your students. Divide them into two reading groups to read it.

Group One

Jesus and His disciples walked down to the lake one night;

The disciples left in a boat and Jesus watched them go out of sight.

Splish, splash, away they went out on the cool, calm lake.

Group Two

During the night a storm came up and the waves on the lake grew rough.

The disciples rowed as hard as they could, but their hard work wasn't enough.

Splish, splash, the waves tossed the boat out on the stormy lake.

Group One

Suddenly, they saw someone on the lake; they were terrified.

"It is I! Don't be afraid," Jesus lovingly cried.

Splish, splash, Jesus was walking out on the stormy lake.

(Continued on the next page.)

Jesus Walks on Water

Bible Story: John 6:16-21 (cont.)

Group Two

They couldn't believe what they saw at first.   How could Jesus be

Walking on the water? An impossibility!

Splish, splash, who was this man out on the stormy lake?

Group One

But Jesus climbed into their boat and before they could say any more,

Instead of out on the stormy sea, the boat was at the shore.

Splish, splash, they got out of the boat and stared at the cool, calm lake.

Both Groups

What amazing miracles Jesus performed that night:

He walked on water and stilled a storm to His disciples' delight!

Splish, splash, seeing Jesus' power out on a stormy lake.

Discussion

- Why do you think seeing Jesus walking on the lake frightened His disciples?

- How did Jesus show He understood their fear?

- Read the memory verse below. We do not always understand God's purposes, but we can trust Him to use His power for us. What are some other "mighty deeds" of God in the Bible?

Memory Verse

"Great are your purposes and mighty are your deeds." (Jeremiah 32:19a)

Jesus Walks on Water

Craft Materials

- patterns on pages 59 and 60
- white cardstock
- crayons, markers, or colored pencils
- tape
- craft stick
- scissors

Craft Directions

1. Copy the patterns on cardstock.
2. Color and cut out the patterns.
3. Tape a craft stick to the back of the figure of Jesus.
4. Cut a slit in the picture using the dashed line as a guide.
5. Insert the craft stick in the slit and hold it in the back, making Jesus walk on the water.

Finished Product

Jesus Pattern

Jesus Walks on Water

"Great are your purposes and mighty are your deeds."
(Jeremiah 32:19a)

Bible Story: John 9

Divide students into two groups: unbelieving Pharisees and the blind man. Have everyone in each group make a sign to hold up: Pharisees—"Jesus is not from God" and blind man—"Jesus made me see." As you tell the story, they hold up their signs at the appropriate times to show the two viewpoints.

One day Jesus met a man who could not see. He had been born blind, so he had never seen trees or buildings or people, not even his own family. Jesus' disciples asked Him, "Who sinned and caused this man to be blind—him or his parents?" Like some people today, the disciples believed that whenever something bad happened to someone, it was because that person had sinned and was being punished by God.

Jesus said, "This man's blindness was not caused by sin. He is blind so God's work can be seen in his life." When Jesus finished speaking, he picked up a handful of dirt and spit in it to make mud. Then he smeared the mud over the man's closed eyes. "Go, wash in the Pool of Siloam," He told the blind man. The man obeyed, and suddenly he could see perfectly!

The man's neighbors were amazed when they saw him. "Isn't that the blind man who used to sit and beg?" they asked.

"No," said others, "it only looks like him." They could not believe the blind man they knew had been healed. But the healed man spoke to them, assuring them of who he was, explaining that Jesus had given him sight.

Some of them took the healed man to the Pharisees, religious leaders, who questioned him about what had happened to him. The man explained what Jesus had done. The Pharisees were more concerned that Jesus had "worked" on the Sabbath by making mud and putting it on the man's eyes! "Jesus is not from God," they exclaimed, "or He would not have broken the Sabbath!" *(Pharisees hold up their signs.)* The once blind man disagreed because Jesus had healed him! *(Blind man students hold up their signs.)*

The Pharisees continued to argue with the man, trying to make him say that Jesus had not healed him. They refused to believe that the man had really been blind. They sent for the man's parents and questioned them: "Is this your son? Was he truly born blind? If so, then how can he now see?"

The man's parents assured the Pharisees that the man was their son who had been born blind, but they would not say who they thought had healed him. "Ask him," they said. "He's old enough to speak for himself."

"Jesus is a sinner," the Pharisees told the man. "He could not have healed you! Only God could do that!" *(Pharisees hold up their signs.)*

"I don't know if Jesus is a sinner or not," the man replied. "I only know that I was blind and He made me see." *(Blind man students hold up their signs.)*

(Continued on the next page.)

Bible Story: John 9 (cont.)

The Pharisees were so angry they began insulting the healed man. Then they accused him of being one of Jesus' disciples. "He could not have healed you," they said. "We don't even know where He came from." *(Pharisees hold up their signs.)*

"That is remarkable," said the healed man. "You do not know where He came from, but He opened my eyes. God does not listen to sinners; He listens to godly men who do His will. If Jesus were not from God, He could not have done this miracle!" *(Blind man students hold up their signs.)*

This made the Pharisees so mad, they threw the man out. Later, Jesus found him and asked, "Do you believe in the Son of Man?" When the man asked who that was, Jesus explained that He was the Son of Man. The healed man said he believed, and he worshiped Jesus. That day the blind man not only received sight for the first time in his life; he also received forgiveness for his sins and eternal life!

Discussion

- What do you think Jesus meant when He told His disciples that the man had been born blind so God's work could be seen in his life?
- Why do you think the man's parents refused to give their opinion about how he received his sight?
- What did the Pharisees want the man to say? Why?
- Read the memory verse below. God's Word teaches us that we need to speak up and say that we believe in Jesus. We should not try to keep it a secret! As the healed man in today's story found out, it isn't always easy to speak up for Jesus. People who do not believe in Him sometimes do not want to hear about Him. Have you ever tried to tell someone about Jesus who did not want to listen? Why is it important to not only live for Jesus, but also to talk about Him?

Memory Verse

"If you confess with your mouth, 'Jesus is Lord,' and believe in your heart that God raised him from the dead, you will be saved." (Romans 10:9)

Craft Materials

- patterns on pages 63 and 64
- white cardstock
- crayons, markers, or colored pencils
- brad fastener
- scissors

Finished Product

Jesus Gives Sight to a Blind Man

Craft Directions

1. Copy the patterns on cardstock.

2. Color and cut out the patterns.

3. Cut out the center of the face.

4. Use a brad fastener to fasten the two circles together.

5. Turn the circles to see the blind man receive his sight.

Front Circle Pattern

Cut out face.

"If you confess with your mouth, 'Jesus is Lord,' and believe in your heart that God raised him from the dead, you will be saved." (Romans 10:9)

Back Circle Pattern

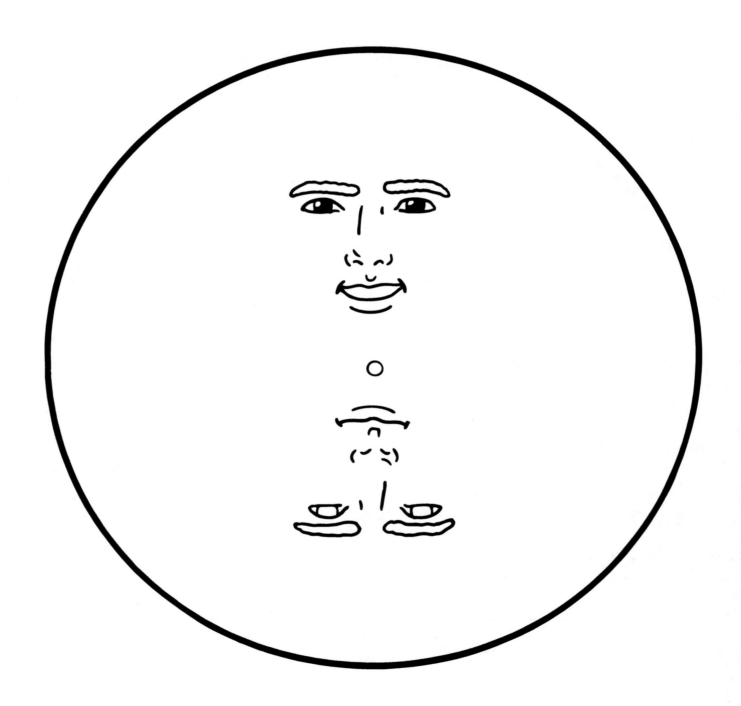

 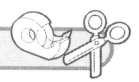

The Transfiguration

Bible Story: Matthew 17:1-8

As you tell the Bible story, draw stick figure scenes on the board and have students copy them.

One day Jesus took three of his disciples—Peter, James, and John—mountain climbing. When they got up quite a ways and no one else was around, an amazing thing happened. As the disciples watched Him, Jesus' face began to shine like the sun and His clothes were white as the light. *(Draw a stick figure Jesus with rays of light coming from His face and body.)*

Peter, James, and John stared in wonder at their master. They had thought they knew Him, but they had never seen Him like this before! *(Draw three stick figures standing and looking at Jesus.)*

Then something even more amazing happened. Moses and Elijah appeared, standing with Jesus and talking to Him! *(Draw a stick figure on either side of Jesus.)* The disciples recognized the two famous servants of God. They had been reading about them all their lives, but had never seen them. Of course not! Moses and Elijah had been dead for hundreds of years. Seeing them talking with Jesus was a miracle.

Peter had never seen such a wonderful sight before. He was so excited, he suggested that he build three shelters—one each for Jesus, Moses, and Elijah—so they could stay right there. *(Draw three tents.)* Peter did not want that thrilling moment to ever end.

But Peter suddenly quit talking when a bright cloud came over them all. *(Draw a cloud over the figures with light rays coming from it.)* and a voice spoke from the cloud: "This is My Son, whom I love. I am well pleased with Him. Listen to Him." The disciples realized they were hearing the voice of God, and they were terrified! They fell facedown to the ground. *(Draw three stick figures lying on the ground, face down.)* Everybody in those days thought if a person saw an angel, he would die. Hearing the voice of God Himself would surely bring immediate death.

(Continued on the next page.)

The Transfiguration

Bible Story: Matthew 17:1-8 (cont.)

Then Jesus came and touched His three friends. "Get up," He told them. "Do not be afraid." Peter, James, and John raised their heads and looked around. *(Erase the cloud and two of the figures. Draw three stick figures on their knees.)* The bright cloud was gone and Moses and Elijah had disappeared. They looked at Jesus and saw that He looked like Himself again. They stood up and looked around in wonder. Had it really happened? Yes, they had seen Jesus "transfigured," changed. He had revealed a little of His heavenly glory to them.

As they went back down the mountain, *(Draw four stick figures walking away.)* Jesus warned them not to talk about what they had seen.

Discussion

- Why do you think Jesus took His three closest friends to a place where there was no one else around for His transfiguration?
- Do you think Peter's idea to build three shelters was a good idea? Why or why not?
- Why do you think Jesus told His disciples not to tell anyone what they had seen?
- Read the memory verse below. When God spoke, no one had to tell Peter, James, and John to bow down; they did it immediately. Why? Why do we honor and show respect to God by bowing down?

Memory Verse

"Come, let us bow down in worship, let us kneel before the Lord our Maker." (Psalm 95:6)

Craft Materials

- patterns on pages 67 and 68
- crayons, markers, or colored pencils
- paper
- glue sticks
- scissors
- cotton balls *(optional)*

Craft Directions

1. Copy the patterns on paper.
2. Color and cut out the patterns.
3. Glue the patterns on page 67 to the picture where indicated.
4. As an option, glue cotton balls to the picture as clouds.

Finished Product

Peter, James, and John Pattern

Jesus Pattern

> *"Come, let us bow down in worship, let us kneel before the Lord our Maker."*
> *(Psalm 95:6)*

Verse Pattern

Glue verse here.

A Rich Young Man Questions Jesus

Bible Story: Mark 10:17-27

Copy the figure of Jesus and the rich young man on page 70 on cardstock for students to color and cut out. Provide craft sticks to glue on the back of the two figures for handles. As you tell the Bible story, let them act it out with the figures.

One day a rich young man ran up to Jesus and bowed before Him with an important question. "Good teacher," he said, "what do I need to do to have eternal life?"

Jesus surprised him by asking a question instead of giving him an answer. "Why do you call me good?" Jesus said. "Only God is good." Then He answered the man's question: "You know the commandments you should obey. Do not murder or steal or commit adultery. Do not give false testimony or cheat anyone. Honor your parents." Of course, obeying the Ten Commandments does not give us eternal life. Jesus was testing the rich, young man to see what he would say.

"I've kept the commandments ever since I was just a boy," the man replied. As Jesus had said, there is no one who is truly good except for God. This young man was certainly not perfect, but he seemed to think he had kept all the commandments perfectly. Jesus loved the man and knew what he really needed.

"There's one thing you have not done," Jesus told him. "Go and sell all your possessions and use the money to help the poor. Then come and follow Me."

Did the rich young man do what Jesus said? No. He was too fond of his possessions. He just could not give them up, not even to get eternal life. The man turned and sadly walked away. He was not willing to even try to do what Jesus said. Jesus watched him go, then said to His disciples, "It is very hard for rich people to enter God's kingdom."

"Then, who can be saved?" His disciples asked Him. They wondered if Jesus was saying that only poor people could be saved.

Jesus did not really answer their question. Instead, He said, "It is easier for a camel to go through the eye of a needle than for a rich man to enter the kingdom of God." That sounds impossible, doesn't it?

Jesus' disciples were amazed at His words. "Who, then, can be saved?" they asked again.

Jesus told them, "With man this is impossible, but not with God; all things are possible with God." Obeying rules, such as the Ten Commandments, does not save a person. Giving up all our money or possessions to help the poor does not work either. The only way to have eternal life is to believe in Jesus and give our lives to Him. The rich young man showed he was not willing to do that when he walked away. He may have wanted to follow Jesus, but he was not willing to give up his riches and put Jesus first in his life. He was looking for an easier way to get eternal life.

Of course, there are both rich people and poor people in God's kingdom because they have put their trust in Jesus instead of in their money or possessions. He is the only way to eternal life in heaven (John 14:6).

Discussion

- Was the rich young man humble or proud? Why do you think so?

- When Jesus said it was easier for a camel to go through the eye of a needle than for a rich man to enter the kingdom of God, was He saying it was impossible? *(No, Jesus may have been referring to another kind of "eye in a needle," a small door within a door, usually part of a city gate. Humans could walk through these small gates, but large animals, such as camels, could not. If the gate was closed and only the small door was open, a camel had to be unloaded of everything on its back—camels were often used as pack animals. Then the camel could kneel down and go through the small "eye of the needle" door. In the same way, a person, rich or poor, must give up the things that are more important to him than Jesus, then kneel down, become humble, to accept Jesus for eternal life.)*

- Read the memory verse below. Believing in Jesus is the only way to have eternal life, but some people just will not accept that. What are some other ways people think they can be saved?

Memory Verse

"And this is his command: to believe in the name of his Son, Jesus Christ, and to love one another as he commanded us." (1 John 3:23)

Rich Young Man Pattern

Jesus Pattern

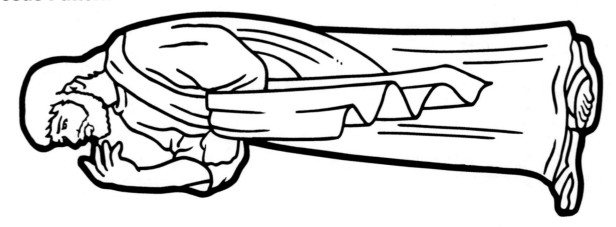

A Rich Young Man Questions Jesus

Craft Materials

- patterns on pages 71 through 73
- white cardstock
- crayons, markers, or colored pencils
- glue
- brad fastener
- scissors

Craft Directions

1. Copy the patterns on cardstock.
2. Color and cut out the patterns.
3. Cut out the "window" on the square pattern.
4. Cut out the art below and glue it to the square pattern as shown.
5. Use a brad fastener to fasten the two pieces together (where indicated).
6. The circle goes under the square.
7. Turn the wheel to tell the story.

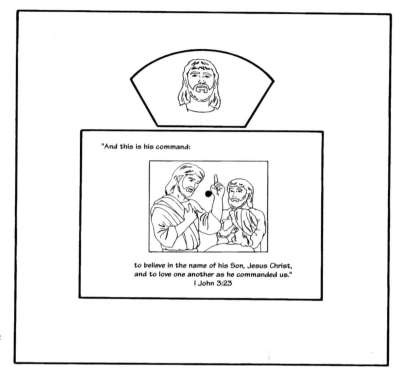

Finished Product

Jesus and Rich Young Man Pattern

Square Pattern

"And this is his command:

Cut this window out.

Glue picture here.

to believe in the name of his Son, Jesus Christ,

and to love one another as he commanded us."

I John 3:23

Wheel Pattern

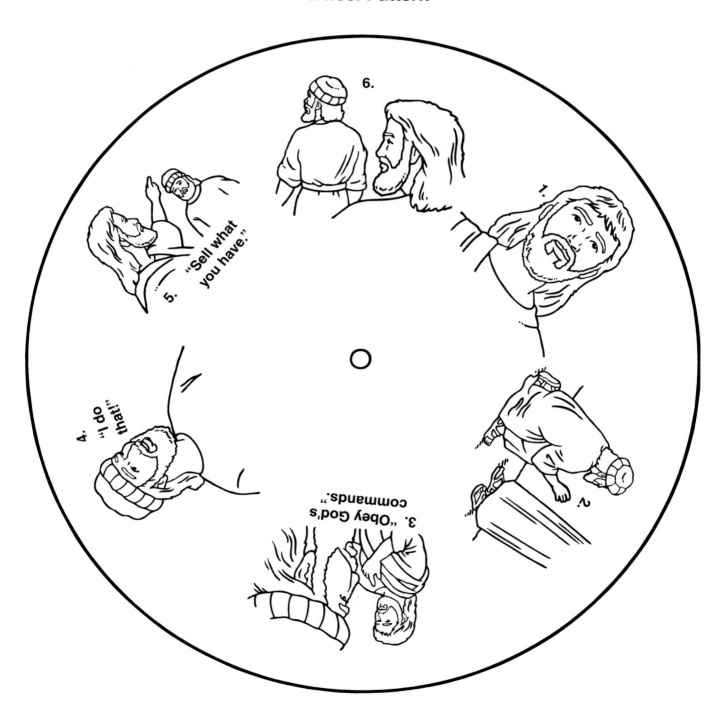

6.

1.

5. "Sell what you have."

4. "I do that!"

3. "Obey God's commands."

2.

Ten Men Healed

Bible Story: Luke 17:11-19

Sing the Bible story song together to the tune of "If You're Saved and You Know It."

Jesus met ten men with leprosy one day.

Only He could make their illness go away.

"Please, help us," they all cried,

For they didn't want to die.

So He told them what to do and they obeyed.

"Show yourselves to the priests," Jesus said.

And their hearts were no longer filled with dread.

As they listened and obeyed,

Their disease just went away,

They were healed from their toes up to their heads.

Only one of the men turned around

And returned to Jesus with a joyful bound.

Kneeling down, he did his part,

Saying thanks with all his heart,

To the Lord and Savior he at last had found.

Only one of the ten returned, it's true,

To do what the rest forgot to do.

He gave grateful thanks and praise

To the Lord without delay,

And he put his faith in the Savior too.

(Continued on the next page.)

Ten Men Healed

Bible Story: Luke 17:11-19 (cont.)

> Oh, the Lord is always doing things for me,
>
> But do I always thank Him properly?
>
> He's helped me so many ways,
>
> He deserves all my praise.
>
> I will praise Him every day thankfully.

Discussion

- Why do you think Jesus told the men with leprosy to show themselves to the priests?
- The one man who cared enough to come back and thank Jesus for healing him was a Samaritan. Most Jews would have nothing to do with Samaritans; they considered them enemies. But Jesus healed both the Jews and the Samaritan. Do you think that had anything to do with the man coming back to thank Jesus for healing him? Explain.
- Read the memory verse below. Why does the Lord deserve our thanks and praise? How often should we praise Him?

Memory Verse

"Enter his gates with thanksgiving and his courts with praise; give thanks to him and praise his name." (Psalm 100:4)

Craft Materials

- patterns on pages 76 and 77
- paper
- crayons, markers, or colored pencils
- glue sticks
- tape or stapler
- scissors

Craft Directions

1. Copy the patterns on paper.
2. Color and cut out the patterns.
3. Glue Jesus to the left side of the page.
4. Tape or staple the right side of men with leprosy pattern to the right side of the page over the thankful man.
5. Lift the flap to show how one man was thankful.

Finished Product

Ten Men Healed

Jesus Pattern

Men with Leprosy Pattern

"*Enter his gates with thanksgiving and his courts with praise; give thanks to him and praise his name.*" (*Psalm* 100:4)

Thank you, Jesus!

Jesus' Story About a Lost Son

Bible Story: Luke 15:11-32

Set up four areas around the room to which you will walk with students as you tell the Bible story. The first area is the home where the story begins. Set up the area to look like a comfortable living room. The second area is the city where the son went. Put pictures on the wall of money, big buildings, and a party. The third area is the pig sty where the son went to work. Put pictures of pigs on the wall and even some stuffed toy pigs or large cutouts of pigs near a feeding trough of some kind. The fourth area is outside the son's home. Mount on the wall the cutout figure of the father waiting with open arms for his son. (Enlarge the pattern on page 79.) As you tell the story, walk students around the room to each area.

(Begin at the first area.) Jesus told the story of a man with two sons. He was planning to leave both of them quite a lot of money when he died. The younger son asked his father to give him his inheritance right away, so he divided the money between the two boys. The older son stayed home and helped his father, but the younger, irresponsible son left home to have a good time. *(Begin walking to the second area.)* He went to a country far from home and spent his money in wild living. *(Second area)* He was reckless and foolish, and it was not long before he had no money left—not a penny! *(Begin walking to the third area.)* He had no friends in that country; they had only stayed with him as long as he had money to spend on them. His family was far away, so he had no one on whom to depend.

(Third area) The son finally found a job, but it was a terrible job—feeding pigs! He had no money for food, and he grew so hungry he actually thought about eating the pigs' food, but he did not dare. No one offered to feed him or help him. That is when the son realized how different his life was than it had been when he lived at home. "Many of my father's hired men have food to spare," he thought, "and here I am starving to death!" He recognized that his attempt to have a good time had ruined his life. He should have stayed home and been a good son to his father.

He said to himself, "I will go back to my father and tell him I know I do not deserve to be treated like a son anymore, not after the way I have behaved. But I will ask him to make me one of his hired men." *(Begin walking toward the fourth area.)* Would his father give him a job? Well, if he did not, the son would be no worse off; at least he would be closer to his family and friends.

He headed for home, eager to see his father and brother, even if it was only as a hired man. *(Fourth area.)* While he was still a long way off, his father saw him and happily ran to welcome him home. He hugged his son and kissed him. "Father," his son said, "I know I do not deserve to be your son anymore." Before his son could finish what he had planned to say, the father told his servants to bring the best robe for his son to wear. The servants brought the robe and put it over the son's shabby clothes. The father told them to bring a ring and sandals for him. They brought a ring and put it on his finger and put sandals on his tired, dirty feet.

(Continued on next page.)

Jesus' Story About a Lost Son

Bible Story: Luke 15:11-32 (cont.)

Then the father told them to kill a calf and prepare a feast. They were going to have a grand celebration to welcome his son home. "This son of mine was dead, and is now alive. He was lost, but now he is found," the father said happily. The boy could hardly believe how his father was welcoming him home. He was being forgiven and welcomed, not at all what he had expected.

The older brother, however, was not so forgiving or welcoming. Jealous of the way his father was treating his younger brother, he refused to come to the celebration. His father went to talk to him, begging him to celebrate and be glad that the lost son had come home.

Jesus told the story of the Lost Son to help people understand that God loves all His children, and is forgiving and welcoming to anyone who comes to Him. In the story, the father represents God and the lost son represents sinners who come to Him and repent of their sin.

Discussion

- Why do you think the father saw his son when he was still a long way from home?
- How did the father show his great love for his son?
- How did the lost son show that he was sorry for what he had done?
- Read the memory verse below. Who is the Son of Man? Who are the lost He came to seek and save?

Memory Verse

"For the Son of Man came to seek and to save what was lost." (Luke 19:10)

Father Pattern for Story

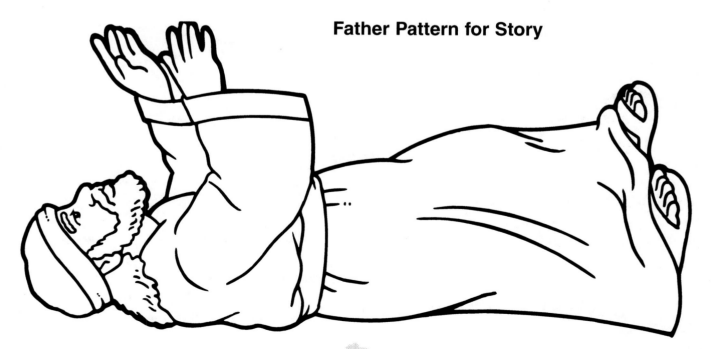

Jesus' Story About a Lost Son

Craft Materials

- patterns on pages 80 and 81
- paper
- crayons, markers, or colored pencils
- glue sticks
- scissors

Craft Directions

1. Copy the patterns on paper.
2. Color and cut out the patterns.
3. Glue the bottom half of the father and the verse to the picture where indicated.
4. Fold the upper half of the father's arms in so it looks like he is hugging his son.

Finished Product

"For the Son of Man came to seek and to save what was lost." (Luke 19:10)

Verse Pattern

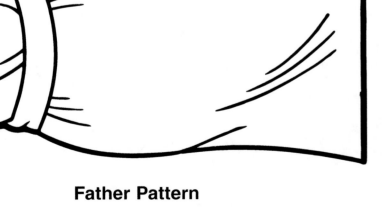

Father Pattern

Glue verse here.

Jesus Enters Jerusalem

Bible Story: Luke 19:28-40

Read the action rhyme and have students copy your actions.

Jesus told His disciples, "Go to that village you see;

(Point to something in the distance.)

Untie the donkey you will find and bring it back to Me."

(Pretend to untie and lead a donkey.)

When they brought the donkey back, they threw their robes on it,

(Pretend to throw robes on the donkey's back.)

To make a comfortable place for Jesus, their Master, to sit.

(Act like you are getting on a donkey.)

He rode the donkey along the road into Jerusalem.

(Make a clopping motion and noise like a donkey walking slowly.)

Crowds of people lined the road, shouting out praise to Him.

(Clap your hands and jump up and down excitedly.)

(Continued on next page.)

Jesus Enters Jerusalem

Bible Story: Luke 19:28-40 (cont.)

> "Blessed is the king who comes in the name of the Lord," they cried.
>
> *(Shout with your hands at your mouth.)*
>
> Some of them threw their robes in His path and ran along by His side.
>
> *(Pretend to throw down your robe and run in place.)*
>
> Some waved branches from palm trees as the crowd's excitement grew.
>
> *(Wave both hands above your head.)*
>
> They praised Him for the miracles that they had seen Him do.
>
> *(Fold hands as if in prayer.)*
>
> Some Pharisees criticized the people angrily,
>
> *(Look angry and shake your index finger as if accusing someone.)*
>
> But Jesus said, "If they keep still, the stones will all praise Me!"
>
> *(Point to the ground.)*
>
> It really was a great parade with excitement all around
>
> *(Wave hands and jump to show excitement.)*
>
> The day that Jesus the Son of God rode a donkey into town!
>
> *(Stand and hold out both arms to symbolize Jesus.)*

Discussion

- Why do you think Jesus chose to go into Jerusalem on a donkey instead of walking? *(Have students look up Zechariah 9:9. Explain that Jesus was fulfilling Old Testament prophecy, showing people that He was the king, the Messiah, for whom they had been looking.)*
- Why were the Pharisees angry at Jesus for letting the people praise Him?
- Could the stones on the ground really praise Jesus as He said? Why?
- Read the memory verse below. Who is the king in this Bible verse?
- God wants us to praise His Son. What are some other praise verses in the Bible?

Memory Verse

"Blessed is the king who comes in the name of the Lord!" (Luke 19:38a)

Jesus Enters Jerusalem

Craft Materials

- patterns on pages 84 and 85
- green paper
- glue sticks
- hole punch
- crayons, markers, or colored pencils
- cardstock
- yarn
- scissors
- paper plate

Craft Directions

1. Copy the patterns on page 84 on cardstock.
2. Copy the palm branches on page 85 on green paper.
3. Color the Jesus and verse patterns, and then cut out all the patterns.
4. Glue Jesus and the verse to the center of a paper plate as shown.
5. Glue the palm branches around the rim of the paper plate.
6. Punch a hole in the top of the plate and use yarn to tie a loop for a hanger.

Finished Product

Verse Pattern

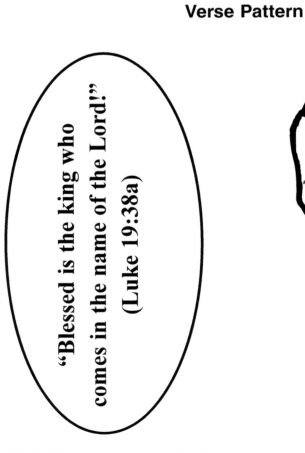

Jesus Pattern

Leaf Patterns

Jesus Talks About Heaven

Bible Story: John 14:1-6; Revelation 21:4-27, 22:1-5

As you tell the story and talk about heaven, list on the board the items in or not in heaven mentioned in Revelation. Have students make their own copies of the list.

The night Jesus was arrested, He had a special meal with His disciples. He told them what was going to happen to Him, which made them sad. Then He said to them, "Don't let your hearts be troubled. Trust in God and in Me. In my Father's house in heaven are many rooms. I am going to prepare a place for you there. One day I will come back to take you there with Me." His disciples were not sure they understood what He was saying. They wondered how they could get to heaven. He told them, "I am the way and the truth and the life. No one comes to the Father except through Me." They could not get to heaven by obeying rules or doing good deeds or going to the right church. They could only get there by believing and trusting in Jesus, God's Son.

Years later after Jesus had died, risen from the dead, and gone back to heaven, His disciple John had a vision of heaven. He wrote what he saw in a book called Revelation. Much of what we know about heaven comes from John's book. The vision he had came from God, and God told Him exactly what to write to let us know about heaven. John tells us what will be in heaven *(Write "In Heaven" as a column heading on the board.)* and what will not be in heaven *(Write "Not In Heaven" as a column heading next to the first one. As you read and talk about heaven, write your findings under the appropriate headings.).*

IN HEAVEN	NOT IN HEAVEN
believers	mourning
	crying
	pain
	temple
	sun
	moon
	anything impure

John said there would be no more mourning or crying in heaven *(Write "mourning" and "crying" under the second heading.)* and there will not be any pain *(Write "pain" under the second heading.).* Can you imagine never feeling pain again? People who have lived in pain all of their lives will suddenly be pain free in heaven. And we will never be sad again when we get to heaven!

In John's vision, there was no temple in heaven. *(Write "temple" under the second heading.)* He said the temple building is not needed because the Lord is the temple. There is also no sun or moon there *(Write "sun" and "moon" under the second heading.)* because heaven is lighted by the glory of God. John also said nothing impure, or sinful, would be in heaven. *(Write "anything impure" under the second heading.)* Only people whose names are written in the Lamb's book of life will be there. *(Write "believers" under the first heading.)* The Bible tells us that when people believe in Jesus their names are written in His book of life.

(Continued on next page.)

Jesus Talks About Heaven

Bible Story: John 14:1-6; Revelation 21:4-27, 22:1-5 (cont.)

John said there would be no curse in heaven. *(Write "curse" under the second heading.)* When Adam and Eve sinned, the earth was cursed, and it has been ever since. But there will not be any curse up there. What will be in heaven is God's throne *(Write "God's throne" under the first heading.)* and God will be seated on it! There will not be any night there *(Write "night" under the second heading.)* but it will be light all the time.

As we look at our list, we have a lot more things listed that <u>will not</u> be in heaven than what <u>will</u> be in heaven, don't we? Maybe John knew that heaven would be too hard for us to comprehend, so he mentioned all the bad things we have in our lives that we would like to be rid of. Can you think of some other things to include in our list of what will be in heaven? *(Examples: angels, Jesus, happiness, love)* There is a lot we do not know about heaven, but we do know it is a wonderful place reserved for those who love Jesus—a place we will enjoy forever!

Discussion

- Who can go to heaven?
- What can we do to help friends and family members get to heaven someday?
- How will our lives be different there? *(Heaven is a holy place with no sin, so everyday life will be holy and perfect with no problems or trouble.)*
- Read the memory verse below. Jesus is preparing a place in heaven for everyone who believes and trusts in Him. How does that make you feel? How can knowing you have a home in heaven make a difference in the way you live your life on this earth?

Memory Verse

"In my Father's house are many rooms; if it were not so, I would have told you. I am going there to prepare a place for you." (John 14:2)

Jesus Talks About Heaven

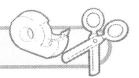

Craft Materials

- patterns on pages 88 and 89
- white cardstock
- crayons, markers, or colored pencils
- glue sticks
- scissors

Craft Directions

1. Copy the patterns on cardstock.
2. Color and cut out the patterns.
3. Glue the patterns to the picture as shown.

Finished Product

Angel Pattern

"In my Father's house
are many rooms;
if it were not so, I would have
told you. I am going there to
prepare a place for you."
(John 14:2)

Verse Pattern

Peter Defends and Denies Jesus

Bible Story: John 18:1-27

Present the Bible story as an interview with students reading the parts: Interviewer, High Priest's Servant, John, Servant, and Peter.

Interviewer: What a night this has been! Jesus, the miracle worker and teacher, was arrested tonight. The high priest's servant was in the group that went to the garden to arrest Him. Tell us about it.

High Priest's Servant: His disciple, Judas, told us we would find Jesus in the garden. We wanted to arrest Him in a place without a lot of people around to cause problems. There were several of us—soldiers, Pharisees, and officials. We carried torches and weapons with us. Jesus came right up to us and did not even put up a fight. Most of His disciples were very quiet when we arrested Him. I do not know, maybe they were stunned. But not Peter!

Inteviewer: What did Peter do?

High Priest's Servant: He attacked us with his sword! I ducked, but he cut my ear off. *(puts hand up to his right ear)*

Interviewer: It looks okay.

High Priest's Servant: It is now because Jesus healed it. He told Peter to put his sword away. He did, and we led Jesus off to be tried for His crimes.

Interviewer: And what were His crimes?

High Priest's Servant: He, uhh, . . . they were . . . . I do not really know; you would have to ask the high priest that question.

Interviewer: Okay, thanks. After Jesus was arrested, He was taken to be questioned. John, can you tell us what happened next?

John: Yes, Peter and I followed our Master. We got as close as we could to see or hear what they were going to do to Him. I managed to get inside the courtyard, but Peter had to wait near the door. He went and stood near a fire with some other men to get warm.

Interviewer: What happened to Peter after that?

John: I don't know; I was paying close attention to Jesus' trial and lost sight of Peter.

Servant: I can tell you what happened; I was near Peter. A girl asked him if he was one of Jesus' disciples and he denied it! Then somebody else asked him the same question, and he claimed he was not Jesus' disciple. I thought I recognized him as the one who had cut off my relative's ear in the garden, so I said, "Didn't I see you with him?" Peter said "no" again. Then a strange thing happened.

Interviewer: What?

(Continued on next page.)

 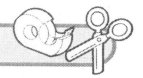

Peter Defends and Denies Jesus

Bible Story: John 18:1-27 (cont.)

Servant: A rooster crowed and Peter began crying, tears running down his face.

Interviewer: *(Peter walks by)* Well, here's Peter! What happened to suddenly make you so sad when you heard a rooster crow tonight, Peter?

Peter: *(sadly)* Earlier in the evening, I told Jesus I was willing to die for Him. He told me I would deny Him three times before the rooster crowed tonight. When I heard that rooster crow, I suddenly realized I had done exactly what He said I would do! I was such a coward! He had done everything for me, and I could not even admit that I knew Him! I felt so terrible I wanted to die. He will probably never want to talk to me again after this!

Discussion

- Why do you think Jesus healed the ear of the high priest's servant?
- How did Jesus show that He understood Peter?
- Why do you think Peter denied knowing Jesus?
- Do you think Jesus forgave Peter for what he had done? *(Have students look up John 21:15–19. The story does not come right out and say Jesus forgave Peter, but it is clear that He did or He would not have given him such an important job to do.)*
- What can we do when we need courage to stand up for Jesus?
- Read the memory verse below. How did Peter sin? Like Peter, we have all sinned. We may not think our sins are as bad as Peter's or someone else's, but in God's eyes all sin is terrible. Sin is disobedience and rebellion against God. What is the only cure for our sin? *(Believing and trusting in Jesus)*

Memory Verse

"For all have sinned and fall short of the glory of God." (Romans 3:23)

Craft Materials

- patterns on pages 92 and 93
- crayons, markers, or colored pencils
- scissors
- cardstock
- glue sticks
- brad fasteners

Craft Directions

1. Copy the patterns on cardstock.
2. Color and cut out the patterns.
3. Glue the verse and the rooster in place as shown.
4. Use brad fasteners to attach the arms to Peter.
5. Raise and lower Peter's arms to show his distress.

Finished Product

"For all have
sinned and fall short
of the glory of God."
(Romans 3:23)

Verse Pattern

Rooster Pattern

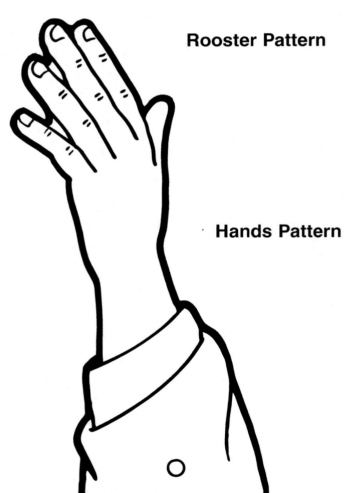

Hands Pattern

Glue verse here.

Jesus' Death

Bible Story: John 19:17-42; Matthew 27:62-66

Since this is a familiar Bible story to most students, let them help you tell it by answering the questions you ask them.

Jesus was found guilty at His trial and condemned to death. What crime had He committed? *(none)* What had He done wrong? *(nothing)* His Jewish enemies turned Him over to the Romans to be crucified. Who carried the wooden cross, on which Jesus would be killed, along the road and up the hill to the place of execution? *(Jesus)* Some soldiers nailed his hands and feet to the cross and attached a sign to it that Pilate had given them. It said: "Jesus of Nazareth, the King of the Jews." The Jewish chief priests did not like that! They tried to get Pilate to change it, but he refused.

While Jesus was dying on the cross, some soldiers gambled for the robe He had worn. Hundreds of years before Jesus had even been born, it had been prophesied that this would happen.

Mary, Jesus' mother stood near the cross, crying as she watched her oldest son die. Even as He died, Jesus was not thinking about Himself. He asked His good friend John to take care of Mary after He was gone.

After hanging on the cross for several hours, Jesus said, "It is finished," and He died. The Jews wanted Jesus taken off the cross as quickly as possible because the Jewish Sabbath would start when the sun went down that evening. They had so many rules about observing the Sabbath, if He was not taken off the cross soon, He would have to be left there until the Sabbath was over because taking Him down would be work and no work could be done on the Sabbath. When the soldiers came by and saw Jesus was dead, they removed His body from the cross.

Two friends of Jesus, Joseph of Arimathea and Nicodemus, came and picked up His body to bury Him. They wrapped His body in strips of linen cloth and placed spices in the wrapping. One of the spices they used was "myrrh." Where have you heard about "myrrh" before? *(The wise men gave some to Jesus as a gift when they came to visit Him when He was a child.)*

Where did His friends bury Jesus? *(They buried Him in a new tomb in the garden.)* The two men worked quickly, hurrying to get done before the sun went down and the Sabbath began. They placed His wrapped body in the tomb and rolled a round stone across the doorway. They just made it.

(Continued on next page.)

Jesus' Death

Bible Story: John 19:17-42; Matthew 27:62-66 (cont.)

Suddenly, it was all over. Jesus was dead and buried. His disciples were scattered all over town. The Jewish religious leaders happily went to their Sabbath preparations, glad to be rid of Him. His friends felt like the world had ended. Was it the end? *(no)* Why not? *(He was going to come back to life.)*

The next day some of the Jewish religious leaders went to talk to Pilate. "Sir," they said, "we remember that while Jesus was still alive He said He would rise from the dead after three days. We think you should have His tomb made secure so His disciples cannot steal His body and tell everyone that He has risen." Pilate agreed. He sent soldiers to put an official seal on the tomb and then to stand guard over it. There was no way anyone could get into (or out of) that tomb!

Discussion

- Have you heard of Nicodemus before? He visited Jesus one night to find out how to be a part of God's kingdom. Jesus' words to him are the first Bible words most of us memorize: "For God so loved the world that he gave his one and only Son, that whoever believes in Him shall not perish but have eternal life." (John 3:16) Joseph of Arimathea was probably a wealthy man and a Pharisee. Why do you think these two men were "secret" followers of Jesus?

- Read the memory verse below. Was Jesus' death forced upon Him or did He choose to die? Why?

Memory Verse

"But God demonstrates his own love for us in this: While we were still sinners, Christ died for us." (Romans 5:8)

Craft Materials

- patterns on pages 96 and 97
- crayons, markers, or colored pencils
- scissors
- hole punch
- cardstock
- glue sticks
- tape
- yarn

Craft Directions

1. Copy the patterns on cardstock.
2. Color and cut out the patterns.
3. Cut a slit on the patterns where indicated.
4. Insert the two patterns together and tape them at the back.
5. Glue the verse to the top of the cross and the heart to the bottom of the cross.
6. Punch a hole in the top of the cross and attach a piece of yarn for a tassel.

Finished Product

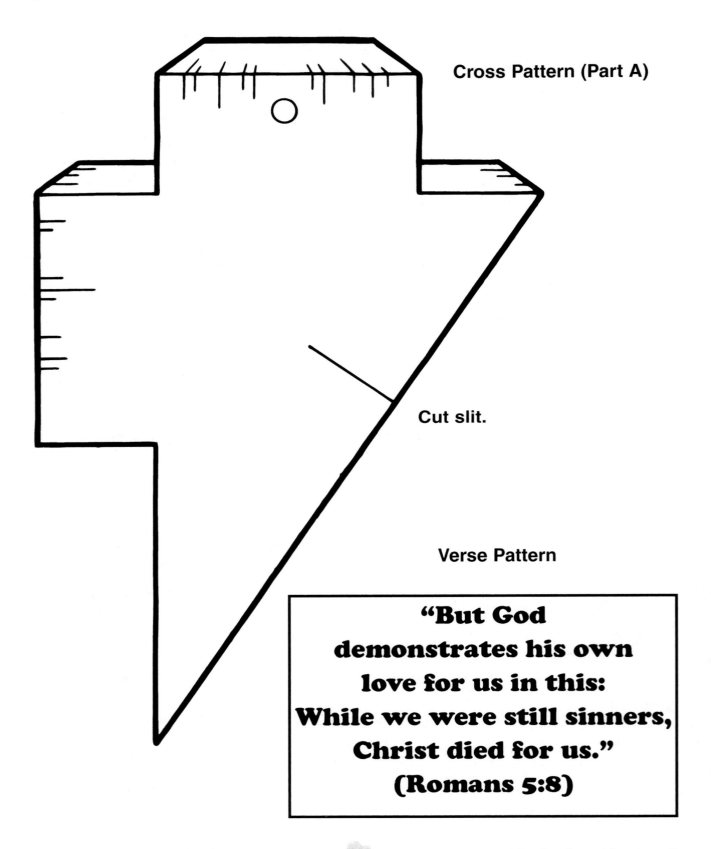

Cross Pattern (Part A)

Cut slit.

Verse Pattern

"But God demonstrates his own love for us in this: While we were still sinners, Christ died for us." (Romans 5:8)

Cross Pattern (Part B)

Cut slit.

Heart Pattern

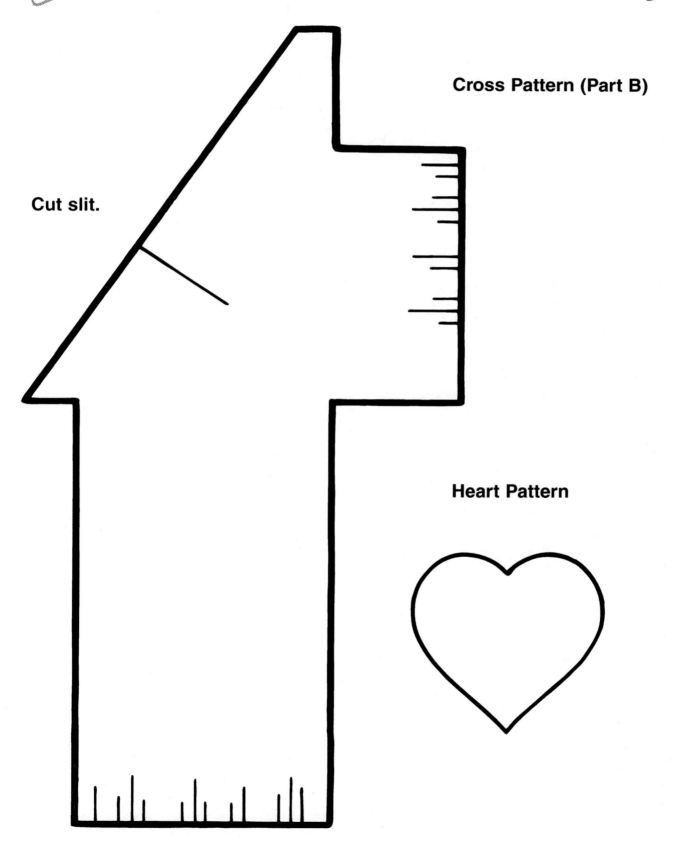

Jesus Comes Alive Again

Bible Story: Matthew 28:1-18

Divide students into two reading groups. Have them read the rhyming story with feeling and enthusiasm.

Group 1

Early in the morning, before the sky was light,

Mary Magdalene went out and saw a scary sight.

Group 2

Jesus' tomb was empty; the door was open wide!

She ran to Simon Peter; "They've taken Him!" she cried.

Group 1

Had someone really stolen Jesus' body in the night?

John and Peter ran back to the tomb in awful fright.

Group 2

There was no body in the tomb, just strips of cloth were there,

The cloth He had been wrapped up in.   All they could do was stare.

Group 1

They did not remember what Jesus Christ had said,

That after dying, in three days He'd rise from the dead.

Group 2

They both went back to their homes, but Mary stayed and cried.

When she looked into the tomb, two angels were inside.

(Continued on next page.)

Jesus Comes Alive Again

Bible Story: Matthew 28:1-18 (cont.)

Group 1

"Why are you crying?" the angels asked. "What is wrong with you?"

"They've taken Him away," she said, "and I don't know what to do!"

Group 2

She turned around and suddenly saw a man nearby.

When He spoke her name she recognized Him with a cry.

Group 1

She saw that it was Jesus, alive as He could be!

"Go tell the others," Jesus said, "that you have just seen Me."

Both Groups

Jesus was alive again! And Mary did just what He said.

She told all His disciples, "He has risen from the dead!"

Discussion

- Why do you think Mary Magdalene went to Jesus' tomb so early in the morning?

- Why did not Peter and John immediately realize that Jesus had come back to life?

- How do you think the disciples reacted when Mary told them she had seen Jesus, alive?

- Read the memory verse below. Jesus did not just die; He conquered death by coming back to life. That is why those who trust in Him are "justified" or saved from our sins. Say the memory verse in your own words.

Memory Verse

"He was delivered over to death for our sins and was raised to life for our justification." (Romans 4:25)

Jesus Comes Alive Again

Craft Materials

- patterns on pages 100 and 101
- crayons, markers, or colored pencils
- tape
- white cardstock
- scissors

Craft Directions

1. Copy the patterns on cardstock.

2. Color and cut out the patterns.

3. Tape the rock over the door of the tomb. Tape it only on the left side.

4. Flip open the rock to read what happened to Jesus.

Rock Pattern

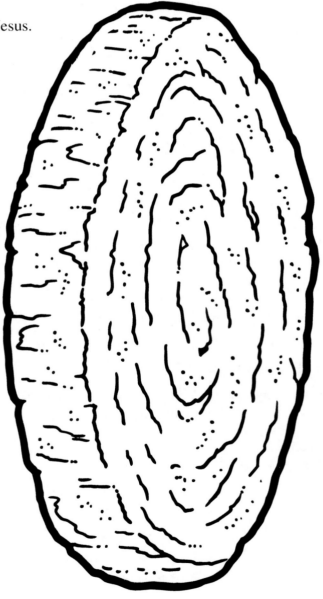

Finished Product

"He was delivered over to death for our sins and was raised to life for our justification." (Romans 4:25)

 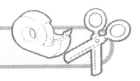

Jesus and Thomas

Bible Story: John 20:19-31

As you tell the Bible story, let students pantomime the action. Choose a student to play the part of Jesus and one to be Thomas. The rest of the group can be the other disciples.

One evening after Jesus' resurrection, His disciples were meeting together. They had locked the doors because they were afraid of Jesus' enemies. *(The disciples huddle close together in fear.)* Would the Jewish religious leaders try to have them killed as they had done with Jesus? The disciples had heard from Mary Magdalene that Jesus was alive, but Peter was the only one who had actually seen Him. None of them knew what to expect next!

Then suddenly, Jesus was there with them. *("Jesus" stands up and holds out His arms.)* They recognized Him and were overjoyed to see Him alive. "Peace be with you," He said to them. Then He held out His hands and they could see the scars where the nails had been. *("Jesus" holds up His hands, then points to His side.)* He showed them the wound in His side where a Roman soldier had thrust a sword into His body. They felt overwhelmed by His Presence. He did not look like a ghost. Was He truly alive again?

"As the Father has sent Me," Jesus told His disciples, "I am sending you." Then He breathed on them *("Jesus" breathes out a loud breath.)* and they suddenly felt different. He had given them the Holy Spirit to give them courage and to help and direct them. *("Jesus" leaves.)*

One of the disciples, Thomas, was not with the others when Jesus came to be with them. They told him later, "We have seen the Lord," *(The disciples talk to "Thomas" excitedly.)* but Thomas did not believe them. *("Thomas" shakes his head "no.")* Maybe he thought they had all had the same vision or dream, but he did not really believe Jesus was alive. He told them he would have to not only see the nail scars in His hands and the wound in His side, *("Thomas" holds out his hands and touches his side.)* but also touch them and feel that they were real before he would believe Jesus was alive.

A week later the disciples were together again. This time Thomas was part of the group. The doors were locked, but Jesus came in without opening them. *("Jesus" comes in and holds out His arms.)* He stood among His friends and said, "Peace be with you."

(Continued on next page.)

Jesus and Thomas

Bible Story: John 20:19-31 (cont.)

Then Jesus turned to Thomas, the doubting disciple. *("Jesus" turns toward "Thomas" and holds out his hands, then points to His side.)* He held out His hands and invited Thomas to touch the nail scars in them. He told Thomas to put his hand on Jesus' side and feel the sword wound there. "Stop doubting and believe," Jesus told him.

But Thomas did not touch Jesus' hands or His side. Now that he saw Jesus with his own eyes, he knew for sure He was alive. He did not need to touch His scars to believe. *("Thomas" falls on his knees before "Jesus.")* "My Lord and my God!" Thomas exclaimed.

Jesus said, "You now believe because you have seen Me. *("Jesus" puts a hand on "Thomas'" head.)* Blessed are those who believe in Me without seeing."

Since Jesus went back to heaven a few weeks later, millions of people throughout history have believed in Him without seeing Him with their eyes. John explained that he wrote the Gospel of John, telling about Jesus' life and death and resurrection so people could "see" Jesus through eyes of faith and believe in Him.

Discussion

- Why do you think Jesus said, "Peace be with you," each time He visited them? *(Perhaps He wanted to encourage them and calm their fears.)*

- What did Jesus mean when He told His disciples, "As the Father has sent Me, I am sending you"? *(When He went back to heaven, they would be the ones to spread the Gospel and do His work.)*

- Read the memory verse below. Why do we need faith to receive Jesus as Savior? Why do we need faith in Him to live our Christian lives? What do you do when you have doubts about God or His Word?

Memory Verse

"And without faith it is impossible to please God." (Hebrews 11:6a)

Craft Materials

- patterns on pages 104 and 105
- cardstock
- crayons, markers, or colored pencils
- tape
- scissors

Craft Directions

1. Copy the patterns on cardstock.

2. Color and cut out the patterns.

3. Fold the envelope pattern where indicated and tape the back and bottom of the envelope shut.

4. Insert the card in the envelope. Pull it out to read the verse.

Finished Product

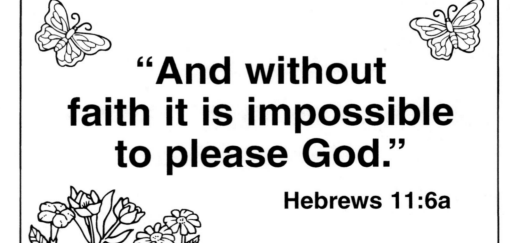

Card Pattern

Envelope Pattern

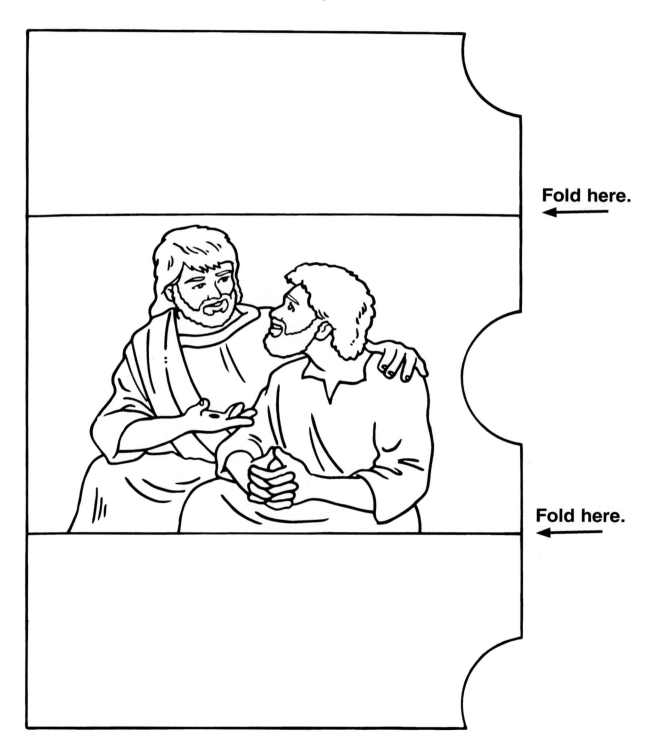

Fold here. ←

Fold here. ←

Bible Story: John 21:1-19

Let students act out this Bible story skit. Choose students to play these parts: Peter, Thomas, Nathanael, James, John, and Jesus. Arrange five chairs together in the shape of a boat. Begin the skit with everyone but Jesus seated in the boat.

John: Boy! What a long night!

Nathanael: Yes, we haven't caught a thing. We should have just stayed home instead of running off with Peter to catch fish!

Peter: Hey, sometimes the fish are there; sometimes they aren't. You never know when you go fishing if you will spend your time hauling in nets filled with fish or staring at the water.

James: *(pointing to shore)* Look! Who is that man on the shore?

Jesus: *(yelling from shore)* Friends, haven't you caught any fish?

Peter: *(yelling)* No, not a thing.

Jesus: Try throwing your net on the other side of the boat, then you'll find some.

Thomas: Who does that man think he is—a fishing expert? We have been throwing the net over both sides of the boat all night!

Peter: Well, it won't hurt to do what he says, I guess.

(The disciples throw the net over the boat, then begin straining to pull in the loaded net.)

John: What in the world? Where did all these fish come from?

Nathanael: Well, they sure weren't there a few minutes ago!

James: It's like a miracle.

John: Wait a minute, I know who that man on shore is. It is the Lord!

Peter: What? *(jumping into the water and swimming to Jesus on shore)* Jesus! Master!

James: *(The disciples row the boat to shore.)* Let's get these fish to shore and thank Jesus for them.

Jesus: *(Jesus welcomes the disciples out of the boat.)* I have made a fire. Take some of your fish over there and cook them for us.

(Continued on next page.)

A Breakfast of Fish

Bible Story: John 21:1-19 (cont.)

(Peter walks to the boat and drags the heavy fish net to the shore. The disciples pick up fish and put them on the fire.)

Jesus: Let's all sit down and have some breakfast.

(Everyone sits down and eats fish. After a couple of minutes, Jesus motions for Peter to follow Him a few feet away from the others.)

Simon Peter, do you love Me?

Peter: *(quietly)* Yes, Lord, You know I do.

Jesus: Feed My lambs.

(They walk a few steps together.)

Peter, do you truly love Me?

Peter: *(louder)* Yes, Lord, I do love You!

Jesus: Take care of My sheep.

(They walk a few more steps.)

Simon Peter, do you love Me?

Peter: *(looking hurt and confused)* Lord, You know all things; You know that I love You!

Jesus: Feed My sheep. Follow Me, Peter.

Discussion

- Since Jesus' death and resurrection, the disciples had spent much of their time hiding behind locked doors. Why do you think they decided to go fishing?

- How do you think John knew the man on shore was Jesus?

- How do you know Peter was excited to see Jesus? *(Peter was the first of the disciples to see Jesus after His resurrection.)* What do you think they talked about? Why do you think Jesus asked Peter the same question three times?

- Read the memory verse below. Peter failed the Lord by denying he knew Him, but Jesus forgave him. How can we have our sins forgiven?

Memory Verse

"Everyone who believes in him receives forgiveness of sins through his name." (Acts 10:43b)

A Breakfast of Fish

Craft Materials

- patterns on pages 108 and 109
- crayons, markers, or colored pencils
- glue sticks
- paper
- tape
- scissors

Craft Directions

1. Copy the patterns on paper.
2. Color and cut out the patterns.
3. Tape the top of the fish net to the picture over the Bible verse.
4. Glue Jesus on the right side of the picture as shown.
5. Lift up the fishing net to read the verse.

Finished Product

Jesus Pattern

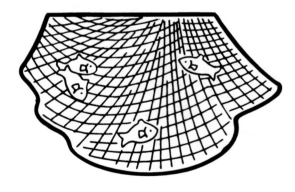

Net Pattern

"Everyone who believes in him receives forgiveness of sins through his name."
Acts 10:43b

Peter Heals a Crippled Man

Bible Story: Acts 3:1-4:31

Give each student a paper plate, colored markers, a wooden tongue depressor, and tape. Let them draw a happy face on one side of the plate and a sad face on the other side, then tape a tongue depressor to it for a handle. As you tell the story, they can hold up the appropriate side of the plate to show when something good or something bad is happening.

One afternoon when Peter and John were on their way to the temple to pray, they met a crippled beggar at the gate. Every day someone carried him to the temple gate so he could beg of those going into the temple. *(Sad face)* When he saw Peter and John, he asked them for money. Peter said to him, "Look at us." The crippled beggar looked at them, hoping to get something. "I don't have any silver or gold," Peter told him, "but what I do have I'll give you. In the name of Jesus Christ, stand up and walk."

Peter took hold of the beggar's right hand and helped him stand. The feet and ankles that had been too weak to be of any use to the man were suddenly strong! *(Happy face)* The man jumped to his feet and began walking as if he had never been crippled! He went into the temple with Peter and John, jumping up and down in his excitement and praising God for his healing. Everyone who saw him was amazed. They were used to seeing the poor beggar sitting by the gate begging, but now here he was jumping around with strong, healthy legs and feet. *(Happy face)*

People came running from everywhere to see the healed man. Peter used the opportunity to tell them about Jesus. *(Happy face)* "You stare at us as if we made this man walk by our own power or godliness," he said. "But it is by faith in the name of Jesus that this man was healed." Peter went on to tell them that Jesus had been killed, but He had risen from the dead. He encouraged the people to turn from their wicked ways to Jesus. *(Happy face)*

Some of the Jewish priests and the captain of the temple guard heard what Peter was saying to the crowd and were very upset. They grabbed Peter and John and put them in jail. *(Sad face)* They wanted to keep them from influencing the people, but it was too late. About 5,000 people believed in Jesus that day. *(Happy face)*

The next day the Jewish religious leaders had Peter and John brought to them for questioning. *(Sad face)* "By what power or whose name do you do this?" they demanded.

(Continued on next page.)

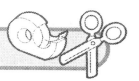

Peter Heals a Crippled Man

Bible Story: Acts 3:1-4:31 (cont.)

The Holy Spirit gave Peter courage to say exactly what God wanted him to say. "It is by the name of Jesus Christ that this healed man stands before you. You crucified Jesus, but God raised Him from the dead. Salvation is found only in Him!" *(Happy face)*

When they saw Peter and John's courage and heard what they had to say, they realized that the two men had been with Jesus. They wanted to prove that what Peter and John said was untrue, but how could they when the healed man was standing right there? The religious leaders sent Peter and John and the healed man to another room while they discussed what to do with them. They decided to warn Peter and John not to speak in Jesus' name anymore. *(Sad face)* But when they had them come back in and told them they must not speak or teach in the name of Jesus ever again, Peter and John did not back down. "Do you think we should obey you rather than God? We cannot help speaking about what we have seen and heard," the two disciples said. *(Happy face)*

The group threatened Peter and John, but could not decide how to punish them or make them stop what they were doing. Many people in the town were praising God for the miracle of healing Peter had done. It was no use denying that there had been a miracle, for the healed man was right there walking around for everyone to see.

Peter and John told their Christian friends how the Lord had worked through them, not only to heal the beggar, but to speak up for Jesus and not back down when the religious leaders threatened them. They praised God together and asked Him to give them courage and boldness to speak His Word. God answered their prayers and the Holy Spirit helped them witness to many people for Jesus. *(Happy face)*

Discussion

- Why weren't Peter and John afraid to go to jail or be threatened by the authorities?
- Did Peter and John ask God to protect them? What did they ask Him for?
- How did God bless their faithfulness?
- Read the memory verse below. Why does it take special courage to obey God rather than people? Where can we get the courage we need to do that?

Memory Verse

"We must obey God rather than men." (Acts 5:29b)

Peter Heals a Crippled Man

Craft Materials

- patterns on pages 112 through 114
- cardstock
- crayons, markers, or colored pencils
- glue sticks
- scissors

Finished Product

Craft Directions

1. Copy the patterns on pages 113 and 114 on cardstock.

2. Color and cut out the patterns.

3. Glue the patterns back to back so that when the gates are opened, you are able to see the verse on the inside. Fold the card where indicated.

4. Copy the pattern below.

5. Glue the crippled man to the left side of the gate.

6. Open the gates to read Acts 5:29b.

Crippled Man Pattern

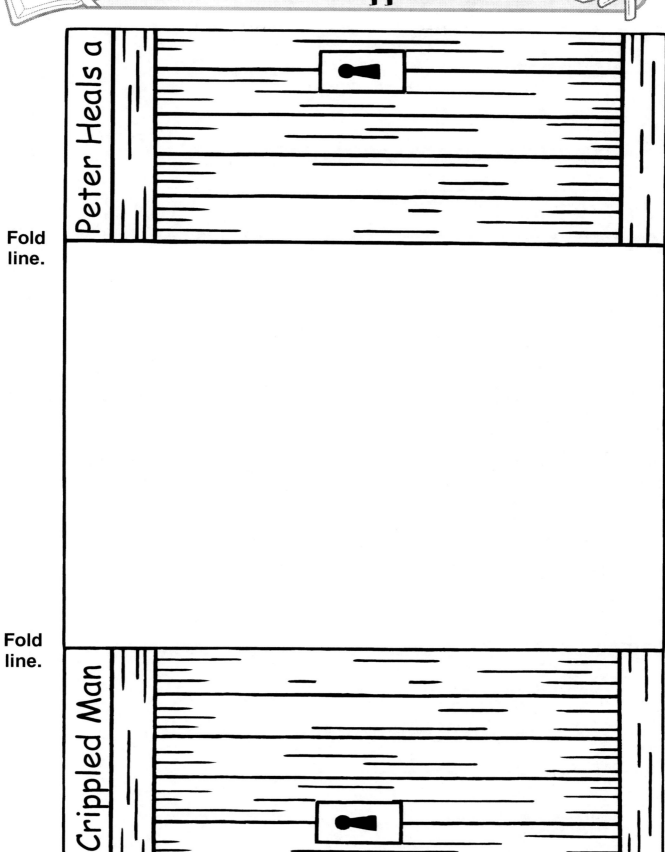

Fold line.

Peter Heals a

Fold line.

Crippled Man

"We must obey God rather than men." (Acts 5:29b)

Bible Story: Acts 8:1-8, 26-39

Let each student choose a partner to act out the Bible story. One can be Philip and the other can be the Ethiopian. Arrange chairs around the room in pairs to represent the Ethiopian's chariot. Begin with one partner in the chariot and the other across the room.

Christians in Jerusalem were being persecuted, so many of them left that city and went to live in other cities and towns. And do you know what the Christians did when they got to their new homes? They talked about Jesus! Before the persecution, Christians stayed together. They told their friends and neighbors about Jesus, but there were many places outside Jerusalem where nobody knew about Him. God used the persecution to scatter His children around to spread His Word.

One of the people who had left Jerusalem was Philip. He went down to a city in Samaria and told everyone he met about Jesus. Crowds began gathering to hear him and God even gave him the power to perform miracles. There was great joy in that city because of the people Philip healed and the people who turned to Jesus.

One day an angel told Philip to go down to a desert road between Jerusalem and Gaza. Philip obeyed, *(Philip walks around the room.)* and on his way he met a man from Ethiopia. The man was an important government official, the queen's treasurer. He had been to Jerusalem to worship. This man worshiped God, but he did not know about Jesus. When Philip saw him go by in his chariot, he was reading God's Word. *(The Ethiopian reads a Bible in the chariot.)* The Holy Spirit directed Philip to go near the man's chariot.

As Philip ran up to the chariot, *(Philip runs in place next to the chariot.)* he heard the Ethopian reading from Isaiah. "Do you understand what you are reading?" Philip asked him.

"How can I understand it unless someone explains it to me?" the man answered. He invited Philip to come into his chariot and sit with him. *(Philip sits in the chariot.)* The man read: "He was led like a lamb to the slaughter, and as a lamb before the shearer is silent, so he did not open his mouth." (Isaiah 53:7b) "Do you know who the prophet is talking about?" he asked.

(Continued on next page.)

Bible Story: Acts 8:1-8, 26-39 (cont.)

Philip was happy to explain the Bible passage to him. He told him that Isaiah was describing God's Son, Jesus Christ. He said Jesus had come to the earth and died for people's sins, then had risen from the dead and was now in heaven. As they rode along the desert road, Philip explained God's plan of salvation to the Ethiopian, and the man believed.

When he saw some water, the Ethopian said to Philip, "Why should not I be baptized?" Philip, understanding that the man had accepted Jesus, agreed to baptize him. The chariot stopped, the two men got out *(The two walk over to an imaginary pool and act out the baptism.)* and walked over to the water, and the new follower of Jesus was baptized.

As soon as the baptism was over, the Holy Spirit took Philip away to another place to preach to other people. *(Philip leaves and the Ethiopian gets back in the chariot.)* The Ethiopian got back into his chariot and headed for home, rejoicing that he was a new man in Jesus! There were many people back in his own country who did not know Jesus. Now he could tell them!

Discussion

- God is all powerful and could have stopped the persecution of Christians in Jerusalem. But sometimes He lets bad things happen, then uses them for good. How did He use the Jerusalem persecution for good?
- How do you know Philip was not ashamed of the gospel?
- What do you think the Ethiopian did when he got home?
- Read the memory verse below. Why do we sometimes act as if we are ashamed of the gospel, not telling anyone that Jesus loves him or her? Whom does Jesus want you to tell?

Memory Verse

"I am not ashamed of the gospel." (Romans 1:16a)

Craft Materials

- patterns on pages 117 and 118
- crayons, markers, or colored pencils
- hole punch
- cardstock
- scissors
- yarn

Finished Product

Craft Directions

1. Copy the patterns on cardstock.
2. Color and cut out the patterns.
3. Place the Bibles back to back and use a hole punch to punch holes where indicated. (Use a little glue to hold the patterns together while punching the holes.)
4. Starting at the top center of the Bible, weave yarn in and out of the holes.
5. Tie a knot in the top of the yarn for a hanger.

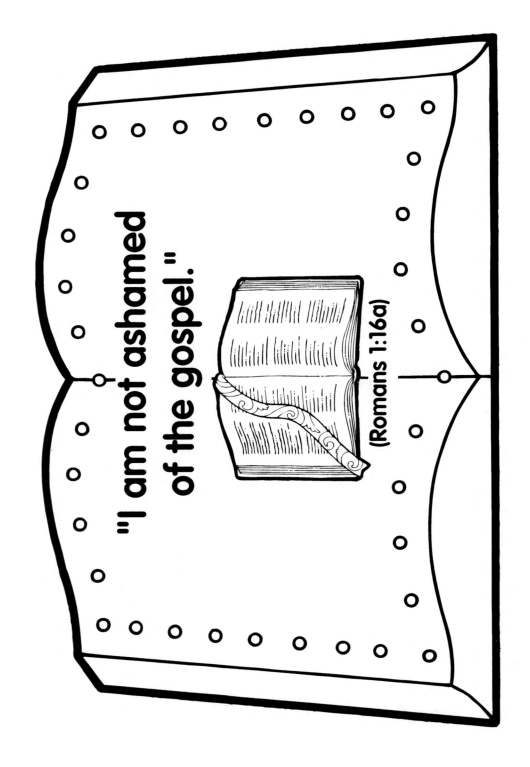

"I am not ashamed of the gospel."

(Romans 1:16a)

Saul's Life Is Changed

Bible Story: Acts 9:1-19

Read the rhyme and do the actions, encouraging students to copy your actions and say the recurring line at the end of each stanza.

Saul persecuted Christians and had them thrown in jail.

(Hold your hands out and shake them in fear.)

He wanted to get rid of them. He vowed he would not fail!

(Hit your palm with your fist.)

Going to Damascus to cause more hurt and strife,

(Walk briskly in place.)

He saw a light and met the Lord, and Jesus changed his life!

(Hold your hands over your bent head as if shading it from a bright light.)

Saul saw a light and met the Lord and Jesus changed his life!

Jesus spoke to Saul that day, became his Lord and King.

(Raise your face and hands toward heaven.)

The men with him could hear the voice, but didn't see a thing.

(Cup your ear with your hand as if trying to hear something.)

Then Paul stood up and turned around, brand new in heart and mind.

(Stand up straight, turn around, and hold out your arms in joy.)

But the others led him to the town, for he was blind.

(Close your eyes and hold out your hands.)

Saul saw a light and met the Lord and Jesus changed his life!

In Damascus lived a man God gave this message to:

(Bow your head and close your eyes.)

(Continued on next page.)

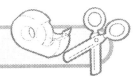

Saul's Life Is Changed

Bible Story: Acts 9:1-19 (cont.)

"You will restore the sight of Saul. Just do what I tell you.

(Touch your eyes with your hands.)

To persecute Christians he has traveled many miles,

(Make a broad sweeping gesture with your arm.)

But now he is My chosen instrument to save Gentiles."

(Cross your hands over your heart.)

Saul saw a light and met the Lord and Jesus changed his life!

After Saul regained his sight, everywhere he'd go

(Cover your eyes with your hands, then remove them and look around.)

He'd tell everyone what God wanted them to know:

(Gesture with your index finger as if making an important point.)

"Jesus Christ, the Son of God, changed my life one day

(Point toward heaven, then yourself.)

And He'll do the same for you if You choose His way."

(Point to others, then toward heaven.)

Saul saw a light and met the Lord and Jesus changed his life!

Discussion

- How did Saul show that He had truly changed after meeting Jesus?
- Why do you think God made Saul temporarily blind?
- For many years, Saul trusted in being good and obeying rules to save him. What did Saul finally learn was the only way to be saved?
- Read the memory verse below. Why is this an important message for Christians to share with other people?

Memory Verse

"Salvation is found in no one else, for there is no other name under heaven given to men by which we must be saved." (Acts 4:12)

Saul's Life Is Changed

Craft Materials

- patterns on pages 121 and 122
- cardstock
- crayons, markers, or colored pencils
- glue sticks
- scissors

Craft Directions

1. Copy the patterns on cardstock.
2. Color and cut out the patterns.
3. Fold the hands in half.
4. Glue the verse inside the hands.
5. Open the hands to reveal God's words.

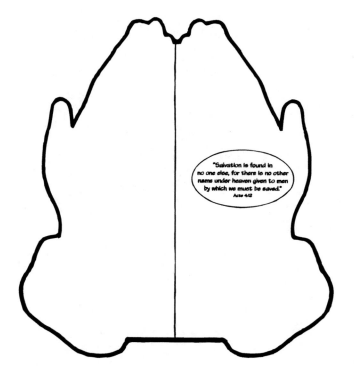

Finished Product

"Salvation is found in no one else, for there is no other name under heaven given to men by which we must be saved."
Acts 4:12

Verse Pattern

Saul's Life Is Changed

Hands Pattern

Peter Escapes from Prison

Bible Story: Acts 12:1-18

Present the Bible story as an interview. Choose good readers to read the following parts: interviewer, Peter, Rhoda, and soldier.

Interviewer: Something amazing recently happened here in Jerusalem! Everyone in the city has been talking about it. Peter, one of the disciples of Jesus Christ, was arrested and put into prison. It did not appear that Peter had broken any laws. Most people say King Herod did it to please some of the Jewish religious leaders who do not like the way Jesus' followers tell others about Him. Let's find out from Peter just what happened. Welcome, Peter.

Peter: Thanks; it is good to be here.

Interviewer: I have heard that the king had you guarded very closely. He must have been afraid you would get away.

Peter: I think so. I was guarded by four squads of four soldiers each. They took turns standing by the doors. When I slept, I had a soldier on each side of me, and my wrists were chained.

Interviewer: If you were that closely guarded, how in the world did you escape?

Peter: Oh, it wasn't anything I did. It was God. I was asleep when a light suddenly shone in my cell, and I saw an angel. He hit me on the side and woke me up. He told me to get up, and when I did, the chains fell off my wrists.

Interviewer: What did the guards sleeping next to you do?

Peter: They did not wake up, not even when my wrist chains hit the floor with a clang. The angel told me to put on my clothes and sandals and wrap my robe around me. Even while I was doing that, my guards did not wake up.

Interviewer: Did the angel lead you out of the prison?

Peter: Yes. I was in a kind of daze, not really understanding what was happening. But I followed him. We passed the first and second guards and came to the iron gate leading into the city. It opened by itself and we walked through it into the street. We walked for awhile, then the angel suddenly disappeared.

Interviewer: Did you come to your senses then?

Peter: Yes. I realized that God had saved me from King Herod. The king had killed my friend James, a fellow disciple, and he may have had the same plans for me. But God rescued me! I hurried to the house of Mary, James and John's mother. I knew Christians would be there praying for me. What happened next was really rather funny.

Interviewer: Let's talk to someone who was there at Mary's house that night. Rhoda, you are a servant in Mary's house?

(Continued on next page.)

Peter Escapes from Prison

Bible Story: Acts 12:1-18 (cont.)

Rhoda: Yes, sir.

Interviewer: Tell us what happened that Peter thinks is so funny.

Rhoda: Oh, it's so embarrassing. Peter knocked on the door and I went to answer it. When I heard Peter's voice, I was so excited I didn't know what to do! I didn't even open the door to him! Instead, I ran into the room where Mary and her friends were praying. I said, "Peter's at the door!" They thought I was crazy. But I said I knew it was him. Someone said maybe it was his angel.

Peter: And all this time I was standing outside the door waiting for somebody to let me in! (*Everyone laughs.*) Somebody finally opened the door and let me in. They were as surprised to see me as this little maid servant was.

Interviewer: Did you tell them what had happened to you.

Peter: Yes, I told them all about it, but I did not stay. I wanted to go and tell my other Christian friends.

Interviewer: We have one more person to talk to about this exciting event. Were you one of Peter's guards in prison?

Soldier: No, sir, I wasn't, but I know those who were.

Interviewer: What did they all think when they discovered Peter was gone the next morning?

Soldier: They were very confused. None of them had heard a thing. They had slept soundly all night. But, of course, they weren't supposed to be sleeping; they were supposed to be standing guard.

Interviewer: Were the soldiers punished?

Soldier: King Herod had them executed.

Interviewer: Oh, I'm sorry. But I am certainly not sorry that you escaped, Peter.

Peter: God was watching over me, as He always does.

Discussion

- Why do you think Peter's guards slept so soundly?
- Why do you think Peter's friends were so surprised to see him?
- When have you been in a frightening situation from which the Lord rescued you?
- Read the memory verse below. What is the most important way the Lord rescues people?

Memory Verse

"'Because he loves me,' says the Lord, 'I will rescue him.'" (Psalm 91:14a)

Peter Escapes from Prison

Craft Materials

- patterns on pages 125 through 127
- crayons, markers, or colored pencils
- glitter *(optional)*
- tape *(optional)*
- cardstock
- scissors
- glue sticks

Craft Directions

1. Copy the patterns on cardstock.
2. Color and cut out the patterns.
3. Glue the wings and the smaller arm to the back of the body as shown. For extra sparkle, add glitter.
4. Glue the halo to the back of the angel's head. Then glue the head to the front of the body.
5. Glue or tape the bigger arm, only at the top over the verse as shown.
6. Lift the arm to read the Bible verse.

"'Because he loves me,' says the Lord, 'I will rescue him.'" Psalm 91:14a

Finished Product

Arm Pattern

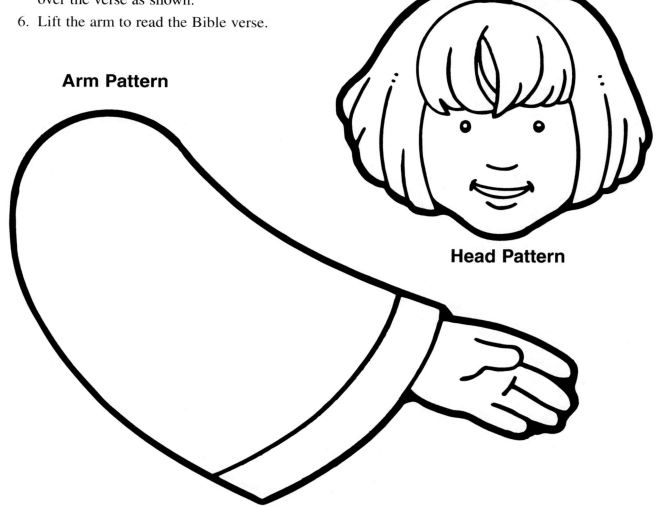

Head Pattern

Peter Escapes from Prison

Body Pattern

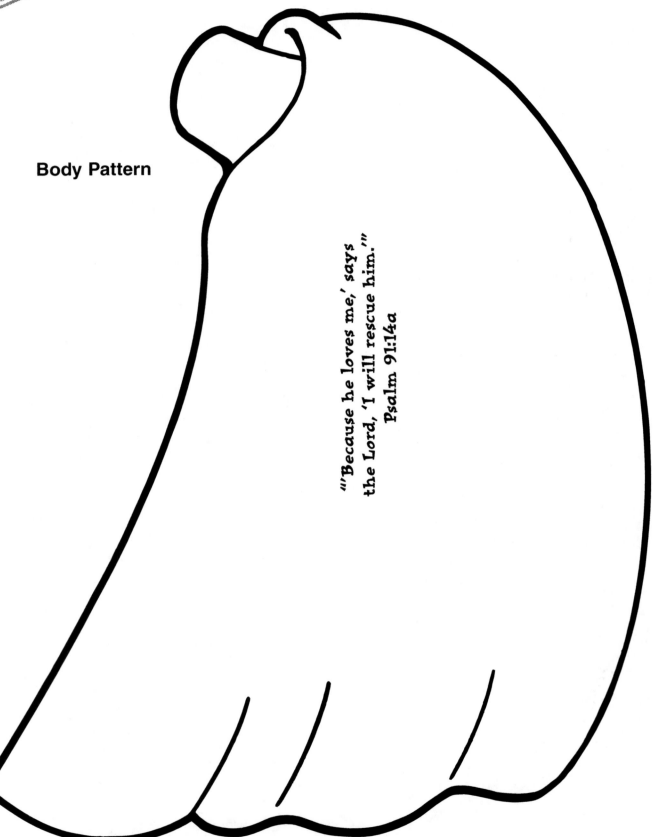

"'Because he loves me,' says the Lord, 'I will rescue him.'"
Psalm 91:14a

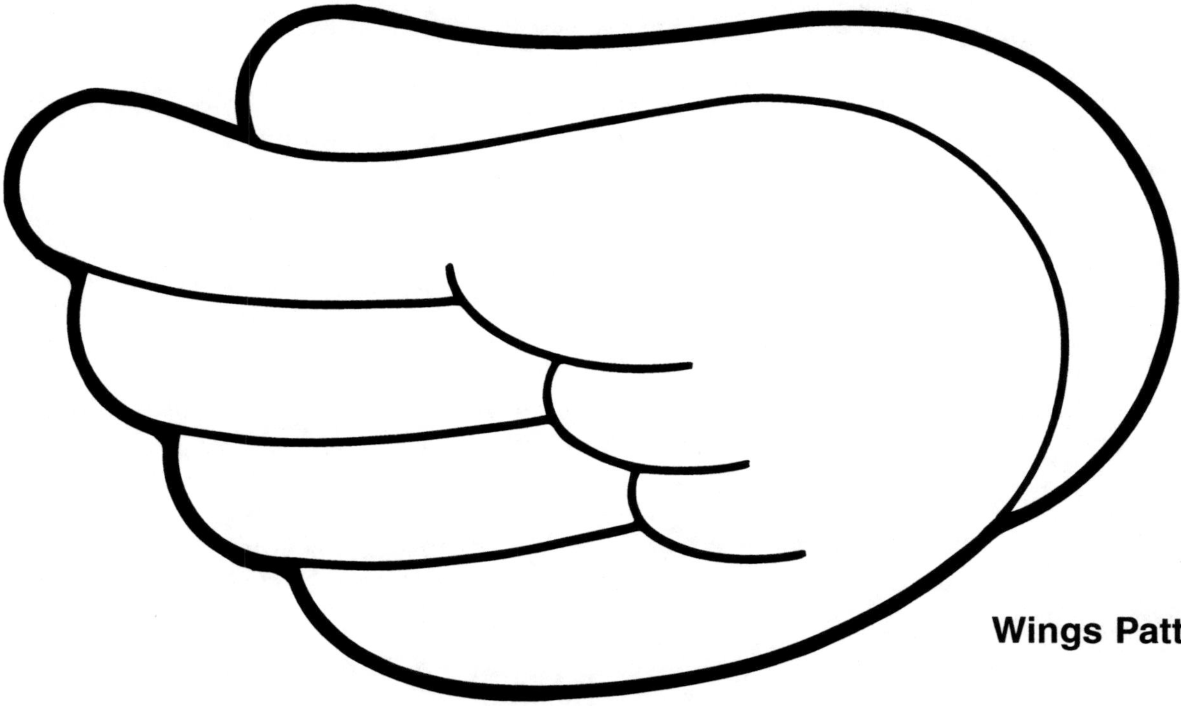

Wings Pattern

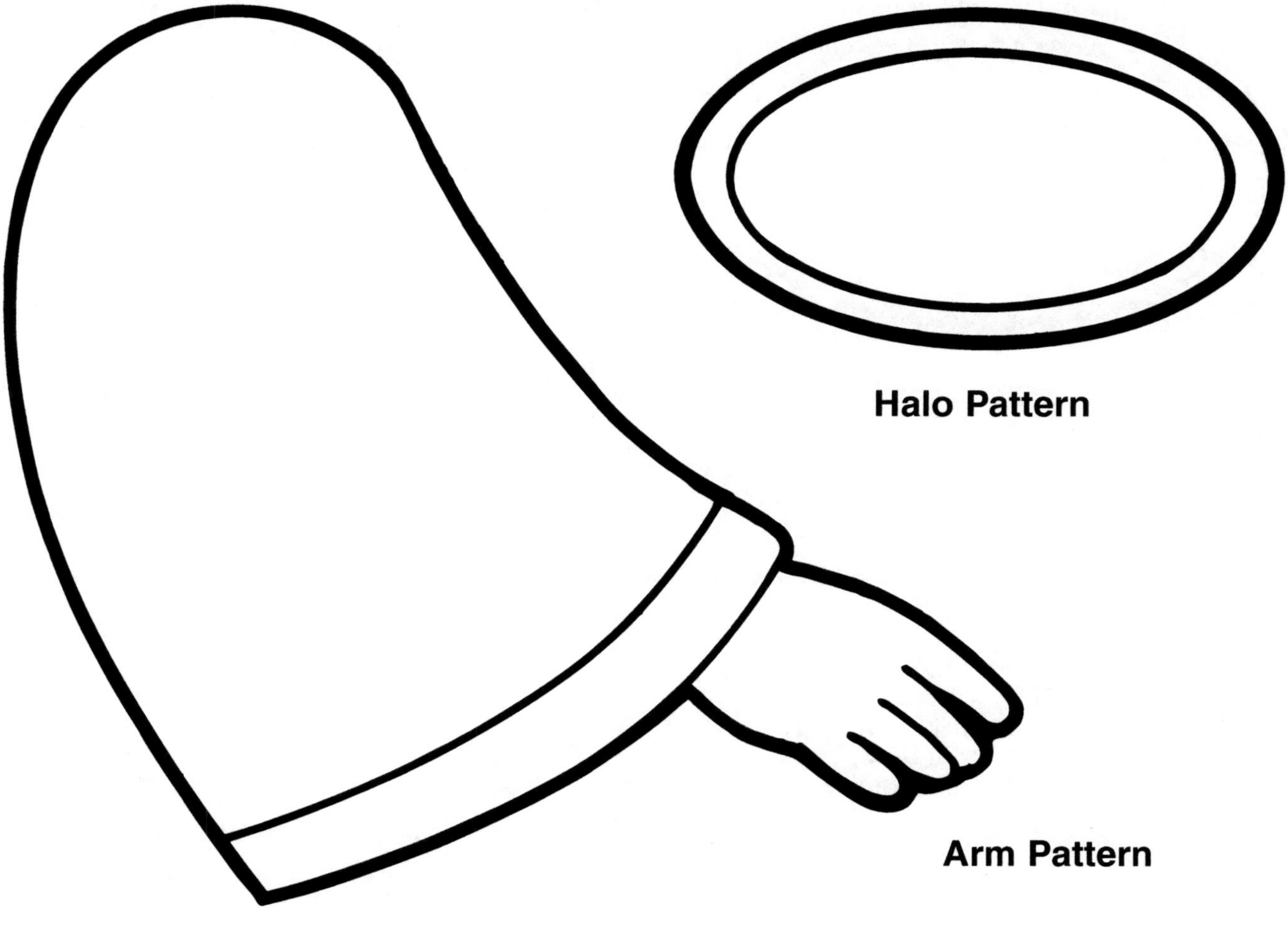

Halo Pattern

Arm Pattern

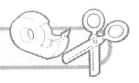

Paul and Silas in Jail

Bible Story: Acts 16:16-40

Present the Bible story as a TV news report. You will need readers for the following parts: News Anchor, Reporter, Paul, Silas, and Jailer. Have the News Anchor sit at a table or desk. Provide a toy or real microphone for the reporter to use.

News Anchor: An earthquake hit the city of Philippi last night, causing some strange occurences at the city jail. We go now to our reporter near the jail for further details.

Reporter: I am standing in front of the jail which looks fine on the outside. We have not been allowed inside. Instead, we will hear from some men who were inside the jail last night when the earthquake hit. Paul, why were you and your friend Silas inside the jail?

Paul: Yesterday, we met a slave girl who was possessed by a spirit that made her able to predict the future. Her owners earned a lot of money by selling her fortune telling services. I called on the spirit to leave her in the name of Jesus, and it did.

Reporter: That was a good thing, wasn't it?

Paul: Not from her owners' viewpoint! After the spirit was gone, the girl could not tell fortunes anymore, so they could not make any money from her services. They were very angry at me. They dragged me and Silas to the police and accused us of going against Roman law. It was not true, but by then an angry mob had formed.

Reporter: So you were put in jail?

Silas: After they beat us!

Paul: The jailer put us in an inner cell and fastened our feet in the stocks.

Reporter: Were you awake when the earthquake hit?

Paul: Oh, yes, in fact we were singing praise to God!

Reporter: You were what?

Paul: We were singing and praying while the other prisoners listened. We knew God had a purpose for us being there. That's when the earthquake shook the jail.

Silas: The amazing thing was that the earthquake did not tear the building apart, but it jolted all the doors and made them open and all the prisoners' chains came loose.

Reporter: I suppose all the prisoners escaped.

Paul: No, I think they were all too startled.

Silas: Then the jailer came rushing in and saw the open doors. He drew his sword, and we saw that he was going to kill himself because he thought all his prisoners were gone.

(Continued on next page.)

Paul and Silas in Jail

Bible Story: Acts 16:16-40 (cont.)

Reporter: Here's the jailer himself. Why were you going to kill yourself?

Jailer: I knew what would happen to me if I presented an empty jail to my captain today! I decided I would kill myself rather than be executed for not doing my duty.

Paul: I yelled to him that he should not harm himself because we were all still there.

Jailer: I called for some lights to be brought in and discovered that what Paul said was true. All the prisoners were there. I knew that was no accident. Some very powerful force was at work. I brought Paul and Silas out and asked them how to be saved.

Silas: We told him how simple it is: Believe in Jesus.

Paul: He took us to his home, and we talked to him and his family about what Jesus, God's Son, had done for them.

Jailer: We believed and put our trust in Jesus—my whole family and I did!

Silas: Then he kindly washed our wounds and fed us a meal.

Jailer: This morning officers came to the jail and ordered me to release Paul and Silas.

Paul: They told us we could go in peace, but I told them we are Roman citizens and we had been beaten and thrown into jail without a trial. I said we would not leave until the head men came and escorted us out.

Jailer: They were scared when they found out Paul and Silas are Roman citizens. There are definite rules about how a Roman citizen is to be treated. I had to laugh when I saw how courteous the police were to them after that.

Reporter: I'm glad your God protected you. Thanks, to all three of you, for sharing your experience with our audience. Now, back to our news desk.

News Anchor: What an amazing story! That's all for now. We'll see you later for the evening news.

Discussion

- The jailer locked Paul and Silas' feet in a clamped down instrument so they could not move them or stand. What do you think the other prisoners thought when Paul and Silas, with bleeding backs and their feet in the stocks, sang praises to God?

- Why do you think none of the prisoners escaped when the cell doors opened?

- How did the jailer show that he was a different man after he believed in Jesus?

- Read the memory verse below. Believing in Jesus means more than just admitting that He was a real person. What else does it mean?

Memory Verse

". . . Believe in the Lord Jesus, and you will be saved—you and your household." (Acts 16:31)

Paul and Silas in Jail

Craft Materials

- patterns on pages 130 through 132
- cardstock and paper
- crayons, markers, or colored pencils
- glue sticks
- scissors
- stapler (optional)

Ankle Strap Pattern

Craft Directions

1. Copy the ball pattern, verse pattern, and ankle strap on cardstock. Copy the chain link patterns on paper.
2. Color and cut out the patterns.
3. Cut the slit on the ball and the ankle strap.
4. Fold the ball in half and glue or tape it together.
5. Glue the verse to the back of the ball.
6. Use the chain links to make a paper chain. Connect the first link to the ball where you cut the slit. Keep adding to the chain. Use the ankle strap to the right for the last part in the chain.

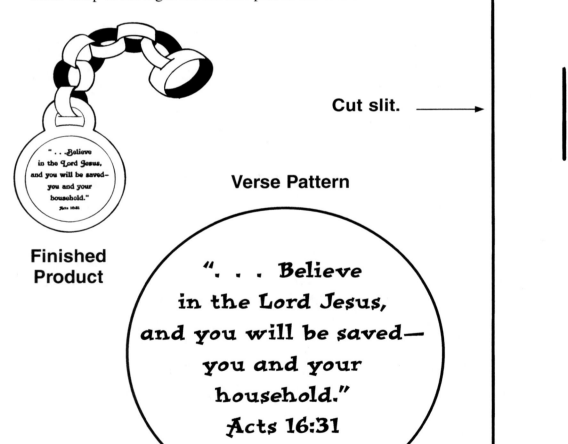

Finished Product

Cut slit. ⟶

Verse Pattern

". . . Believe
in the Lord Jesus,
and you will be saved—
you and your
household."
Acts 16:31

Paul and Silas in Jail

Chain Link Patterns

Ball Pattern

Cut slit.

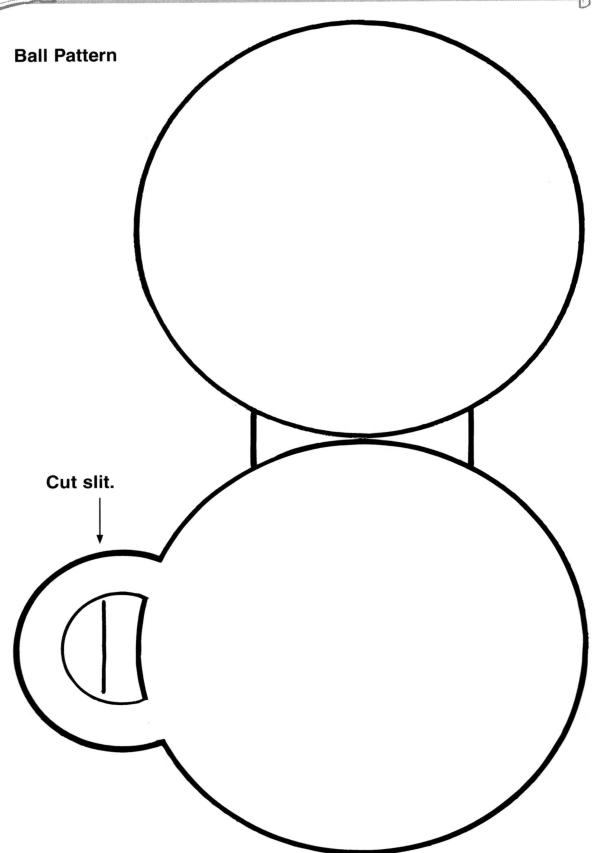

Paul in Jerusalem

Bible Story: Acts 21:1-23:11

As you tell the Bible story, draw stick figures on the board and have students copy them to illustrate what happened.

Paul was headed for Jerusalem. *(Draw a stick figure Paul.)* He had traveled over most of Israel and the surrounding countries to tell people about Jesus. Now, he felt the Holy Spirit was leading him to Jerusalem. Friends warned him not to go. He had enemies there who wanted to get rid of him. The Holy Spirit had already let Paul know that he would face trouble and even prison in the weeks and months ahead, but that did not stop him. He wanted to be where God wanted him!

He got on a ship and headed out. *(Draw a stick figure in a sailing ship.)* When the ship stopped at places along the way, Paul got off and spent time with Christians in each place. They were worried about what would happen to him in Jerusalem. But he said, "I am ready to die in Jerusalem for the name of Jesus." They agreed with him that he needed to do God's will. Then he got back on the ship to continue his trip.

When Paul arrived in Jerusalem, the Christians there greeted him warmly. *(Draw one stick figure hugging another.)* He told them all about what God had been doing on his missionary trips. Most of his work had been with Gentiles. The people warned him that some Jews in the city were angry that he had been preaching God's Word to Gentiles. Many Jews hated Gentiles. If they saw a Gentile walking toward them, they would cross the street to avoid him!

Things were calm for a few days, then some Jews saw Paul at the temple, and they grabbed him and stirred up a crowd against him. They accused him of defiling the temple, which was not true. People came running from all directions when they heard the noise. *(Draw a crowd of stick figures with Paul in the middle.)* Paul's life was in danger when someone told the Roman commander what was happening. He took some other officers and ran to the scene. When the rioters saw the soldiers coming, they stopped beating Paul.

The commander arrested Paul and put him in chains. When he asked who Paul was and what he had been doing, angry people in the crowd started yelling accusations against him. The commander could not understand, so he took Paul to the barracks where the soldiers stayed. The soldiers had to carry Paul to keep him from being torn apart. *(Draw stick figure Paul being carried.)* "Away with him!" the Jews kept shouting.

(Continued on next page.)

Paul in Jerusalem

Bible Story: Acts 21:1-23:11 (cont.)

As the soldiers were carrying Paul inside, he asked the commander if he could speak to the crowd. As soon as he was given permission, Paul stood on the steps and began telling about how God had used him. *(Draw stick figure Paul preaching.)* The rioters grew quiet as they listened to him. He told how he had persecuted Christians until he met Jesus. But when Paul said that God had sent him to be a missionary to Gentiles, the crowd got angry again and shouted, "Rid the earth of him! He's not fit to live!"

The commander rushed Paul into the barracks and closed the door. He ordered that Paul be beaten and questioned. "Is it legal for you to beat a Roman citizen?" Paul asked. The commander was worried. *(Draw stick figure Paul and a soldier stick figure.)* It was the law that Roman citizens were to be treated fairly, not beaten or arrested for no reason.

The next day the commander took Paul before the Sanhedrin, a group of Jewish religious leaders. Paul talked to them about Jesus. *(Draw stick figure Paul speaking to a group of stick figures.)* When he mentioned Jesus' resurrection, he caused an uproar because some of the men on the Sanhedrin believed in the resurrection and some did not. They began to argue and became so violent that the commander had to take Paul back to the barracks to keep him from being killed.

The following night God said to Paul, "Take courage. You have spoken of Me in Jerusalem and you will speak of Me in Rome." *(Draw cloud with God's words in it above stick figure Paul.)*

Discussion

- Why do you think so many of the Jews wanted to kill Paul? Was Paul worried? Why not?
- Why do you think God's message to Paul was an encouragement?
- Read the memory verse below. What is a fortress? What is a refuge? Who takes care of us that way?

Memory Verse

"For you are my fortress, my refuge in times of trouble." (Psalm 59:16b)

Paul in Jerusalem

Craft Materials

- patterns on pages 135 and 136
- cardstock
- hole punch
- crayons, markers, or colored pencils
- glue sticks
- scissors
- yarn

Craft Directions

1. Copy the patterns on cardstock.
2. Color and cut out the patterns.
3. Glue Paul in the prison scene where shown.
4. Punch holes in the top and bottom of the prison scene where indicated.
5. Insert yarn to make the prison bars.

Paul Pattern

"For you are my fortress, my refuge in times of trouble." Psalm 59:16b

Finished Product

Paul Preaches to a King

Bible Story: Acts 24-26

Make four paper signs with the following words on them: 1. Later! 2. Send him to Caesar! 3. You're crazy! 4. He should be set free. Choose students to hold up the signs so everyone can see how different people responded to Paul when you call on them as you tell the Bible story.

Paul was in jail. He had been arrested in Jerusalem after an angry mob of Jews tried to kill him. They accused him of going against Roman law, but no one had proved it. He was kept in jail until the Roman commander heard about a plot to kill Paul. He decided to take him to Caesarea to avoid murder. Now in Caesarea, Paul was being kept under guard in the palace waiting to be tried. Governor Felix said he would hear his case when Paul's accusers arrived from Jerusalem.

Five days later Jewish religious leaders arrived from Jerusalem and met with Governor Felix and Paul. Their lawyer presented their charges against Paul to the governor. "He is a troublemaker, stirring up trouble all over the world! He caused a riot and defiled our temple," the lawyer said. Governor Felix did not seem to be impressed. He let Paul respond to their accusations. Paul pointed out that they could not prove he had done anything against Roman law. He said his conscience was clear before God.

It turned out that the governor knew about Jesus and the people who followed Him. He did not really see any reason to condemn Paul, so he told him he would decide a verdict when the Roman commander who had arrested Paul came. *(Have a student stand and hold up the "Later" sign.)* Felix ordered that Paul be allowed some freedom and his friends could visit him and take care of his needs. Several days later, the governor came with his wife to meet with Paul again. Paul shared more of God's truth with him. Once again Governor Felix told Paul he would decide his case later. The governor's visits with Paul went on for two years without a verdict ever being given. *(The "Later" student sits down.)*

Two years later, Governor Felix was replaced by Governor Festus. One day the new governor went to Jerusalem. When the Jewish religious leaders heard he was there, they went to him and presented their charges against Paul. They asked him to transfer Paul to Jerusalem because they secretly planned to kill him. Festus would not agree, but he invited them to come to Caesarea and present their charges again. The Jews came and met with Festus and Paul. Again they presented their charges, none of which they could prove.

Paul defended himself. Then Festus, wanting to do the Jews a favor, asked Paul, "Are you willing to go up to Jerusalem and stand trial before me on these charges?" Paul refused, knowing they would kill him. Instead, he requested that he be sent to Rome to stand trial before Caesar. The governor replied, "You have appealed to Caesar. To Caesar you will go!" *(Have a student stand and hold up the "Send him to Caesar!" sign, then sit back down.)*

A few days later King Agrippa came to town. Governor Festus discussed Paul's case with the king. "His accusers did not charge him with any of the crimes I expected," he said. "They were just religious disputes. I wasn't sure how to investigate the matter." Then he appealed to Caesar himself. King Agrippa was interested and decided he would like to hear what Paul had to say.

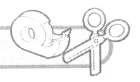

Paul Preaches to a King

Bible Story: Acts 24-26 (cont.)

The next day King Agrippa and Governor Festus met with Paul. The room was filled with people—high-ranking officers and the leading men of the city. Festus told everyone why Paul was there. "I am going to send him to Rome," he said, "but I have nothing definite to write to His Majesty about him. I have brought him before you so that as a result of this investigation I may have specific charges to write against him."

King Agrippa said to Paul, "You have permission to speak for yourself."

Paul began to talk. He wasn't afraid to speak up no matter how many important people were in the room. He told them all how he had been raised to be a dedicated Jew, so dedicated in fact, that he chased down and persecuted Christians because he believed they were wrong and a threat to the Jewish religion. Then he described how he had met Jesus one day and realized how wrong he had been. He explained that God had been using him to spread His message of love to Gentiles wherever he went. "I preached that they should repent and turn to God," he said. "That is the real reason the Jews seized me in the temple courts and tried to kill me." Then Paul told them how Jesus had died and risen from the dead for them.

"You're crazy, Paul!" Governor Festus exclaimed. *(Have a student stand and hold up the "You're crazy!" sign, then sit back down.)* Paul went on talking, appealing to King Agrippa who, he felt, believed what he was saying.

When Paul was finished, the king and the governor left the room and discussed his case. "This man has done nothing that deserves imprisonment or death," King Agrippa said. "He should be set free, *(Have a student stand and hold up the "He should be set free" sign, then sit back down.)* but since he has appealed to Caesar, he must be sent to Rome." *(Have a student stand and hold up the "Send him to Caesar!" sign.)* So that is where Paul would be sent, exactly where he wanted to go to be a witness for the Lord!

Discussion

- What did Paul talk about every time he was given an opportunity to speak to someone?
- Why do you think the Jewish religious leaders got so angry at what Paul had to say?
- How was God watching over Paul and caring for him?
- Read the memory verse below. What does it mean to be prepared to preach the Word "in season and out of season"? Who should be prepared to do this?

Memory Verse

"Preach the Word; be prepared in season and out of season." (2 Timothy 4:2a)

Paul Preaches to a King

Craft Materials

- patterns on pages 139 and 140
- cardstock
- crayons, markers, or colored pencils
- glue sticks
- scissors
- sequins

Finished Product

Craft Directions

1. Copy the patterns on cardstock.
2. Color and cut out the patterns.
3. Fold the crown in half.
4. Glue the verse to the inside of the crown.
5. Decorate the crown with sequins.

Verse Pattern

"Preach the Word;
be prepared in season
and out of season."
2 Timothy 4:2a

Crown Pattern

A Trip to Rome

Bible Story: Acts 27-28

Sing the Bible story song together to the tune of "On Top of Old Smokey."

Paul went on a boat ride,
He sailed far from home.
Each passenger sailing
Was a prisoner of Rome.

A soldier named Julius
Was in charge of them all.
He treated them kindly,
Especially Paul.

The winds were against them;
Their progress was slow.
Paul warned them to stop, but
The ship's pilot said, "go!"

A storm tossed and battered
The ship day and night.
They thought they would all drown,
They were all filled with fright.

But God spoke to Paul and
Said, "Don't be afraid.
You'll land on an island;
Everyone will be saved."

(Continued on next page.)

A Trip to Rome

Bible Story: Acts 27–28 (cont.)

> The wind blew the ship to
> An island nearby.
> Everyone swam and
> Not one person died.
>
> The islanders welcomed
> The men to their home.
> Then three months later,
> They went on to Rome.
>
> Paul lived in a house with
> A guard always near.
> Speaking of Jesus
> To all who would hear.

Discussion

- How did God show He was watching over Paul and taking care of him?
- When he first got to the island, a poisonous snake bit Paul and it didn't even make him sick. The islanders were amazed and thought he was some kind of god. Later, Paul healed many sick people on the island, which must have made them think he was a very powerful god! How do you think Paul responded when the people called him a god? What did he tell them?
- Read the memory verse below. Does God have good plans or bad plans for you? What do you think "plans to prosper you" means? What is the hope and future God has for each of His children?

Memory Verse

"'For I know the plans I have for you,' declares the Lord, 'plans to prosper you and not to harm you, plans to give you hope and a future.'" (Jeremiah 29:11)

A Trip to Rome

Craft Materials

- patterns on pages 143 and 144
- cardstock
- crayons, markers, or colored pencils
- glue sticks
- scissors
- rubber bands or string

Craft Directions

1. Copy the patterns on cardstock.
2. Color and cut out the patterns.
3. Glue the scroll rods to the back of the scroll.
4. Glue the dove to the top right corner of the scroll as shown.
5. Roll the ends of the scroll together and use rubber bands or string to hold it together.

Scroll Rod Patterns

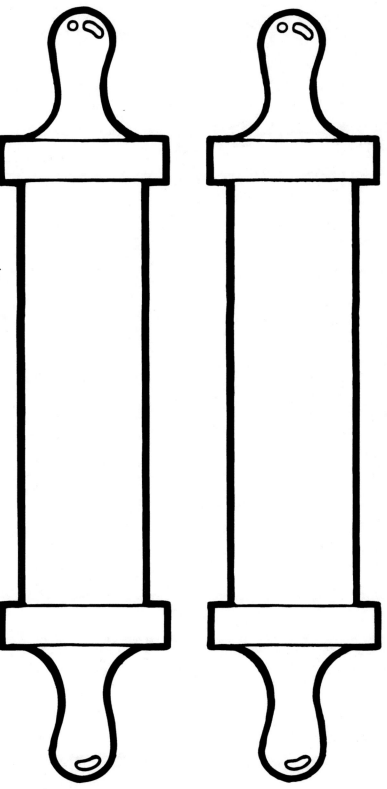

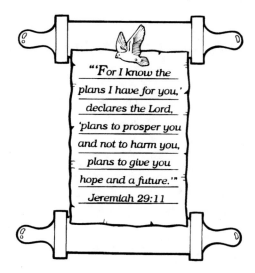

"'For I know the plans I have for you,' declares the Lord, 'plans to prosper you and not to harm you, plans to give you hope and a future.'"
Jeremiah 29:11

Finished Product

Dove Pattern

Scroll Pattern

"'For I know the plans I have for you,' declares the Lord, 'plans to prosper you and not to harm you, plans to give you hope and a future.'"
Jeremiah 29:11